CYNTHIA HEIMEL

SIMON AND SCHUSTER, NEW YORK

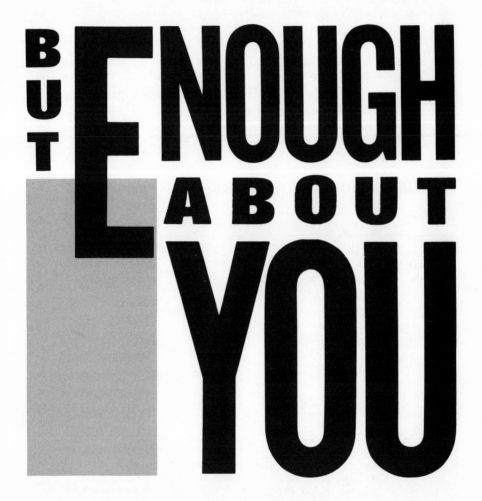

MANUFACTURED IN THE UNITED STATES OF AMERICA

10 9 8 7 6 5 4 3 2 1

LIBRARY OF CONGRESS CATALOGING-IN-PUBLICATION DATA
HEIMEL, CYNTHIA, DATE—
     BUT ENOUGH ABOUT YOU.

     I. TITLE.
PN6162.H394   1986   814'.54   86-15594.
ISBN: 0-671-55264-3

"When in Doubt, Act Like Myrna Loy" originally published in *Vogue*.
Courtesy *Vogue*. Copyright © 1984 by The Condé Nast Publications,
Inc. "Help, I'm a Yuppie" copyright © 1984. The Hearst Corpora-
tion. Courtesy *Harper's Bazaar*. Several of the other columns origi-
nally appeared in *The Village Voice*. Reprinted with permission of
The Village Voice.

FOR BRODIE R. HEIMEL,

IN THE HOPE
THAT SOMEDAY
HE MAY DECIDE
HE LIKES
TO READ

CONTENTS

PART ONE: FABULOUSNESS

PART TWO: OUTFITS

PART THREE: URBANITY

PART FOUR: LOVE AFFAIRS

FABULOUSNESS

AVOIDING FABULOUSNESS

Aren't we sick to death of picking up a magazine and reading again about how this has been the "greed" decade? Don't we sit around stifling yawns as our eyes glance off editorials denouncing money-grubbing and pathological self-interest? Aren't we bored?

Don't we know that it's not greediness that is curdling the minds of the citizenry, but fabulousness?

Fab′u•lous•ness the desire at all times to eat fabulous food at fabulous restaurants while wearing fabulous clothes and chatting with fabulous people after kissing the fabulous maitre d' on both cheeks so he'll show you to a fabulous table, and before going off (maybe in a fabulous limo, although that may be *too* fabulous to be fabulous) to a fabulous nightclub where the doormen all know you (kiss kiss) and the crowds part for you and several free-drink tickets are pressed into your fabulously manicured hand as you make your unfettered way to the V.I.P. room which actually has a special row of V.V.I.P. couches where no one can sit but you, a movie star, an MTV personality, and a fabulously famous model with a cockatoo.

The closest 99 percent of us actually get to this kind of fabulousness is sneaking a read of *People* (Princess Di's secret life! Cher has an eyelid job!) at the corner newsstand before the man tells us we're not in a library. But all Americans, plus many Europeans, Asians, and Africans, have a sneaky little need to be fabulous, even if we're farmers in Idaho and have never even heard of Cybill Shepherd. It's nothing to be ashamed of.

It started, as everything inevitably does, in the sandbox, when we were happily constructing sand pies and minding our own business until some incredibly offensive girl in a pink pinafore kicked sand into our eyes. It hurt, we couldn't see, we began crying, all the other children started snickering, and the desire for fabulousness was born. "I'll show you, you jelly-smeared little maggots!" we shrieked in miserable fury. "One day, when we're all grown up and you're all selling insurance in Peoria, I will be lunching every day in my own booth at the Russian Tea Room! With my agent!"

The desire for fabulousness reached its peak in the high school cafeteria, as we stood there with our tray of mystery meat and milk, the hormones surging through our blood and our knee socks hanging limply about our ankles, and saw the captain of the football team throwing pieces of roll at the girl with the long blond hair and the huge knockers, and the awful realization hit us that *he would never be ours.*

Sex starvation and wounded dignity are at the root of all fabulousness. Although some authorities believe that fabulousness is caused by a germ that was first isolated in Westhampton, New York.

We must all take care. Although we know that there is a dark, fetid part of each of our souls that cries out for it, we must never take that wild, demented, crucial step and give ourselves totally to the headlong pursuit of fabulousness.

If steps aren't taken, if fabulousness cravings aren't checked, the entire fabric of society will be irrevocably rent. Where there are now corner luncheonettes, there will soon be bistros selling only sun-dried tomatoes, smoked mozzarella, and lemon Perrier. Every dry cleaner will be replaced with yet another branch of

Benetton, every drugstore will be transformed into a
nightclub with a stringent door policy. It could get
ugly!

IS IT TOO LATE? HAVE I ALREADY COMPLETELY SUCCUMBED TO FABULOUSNESS?

TAKE THIS SIMPLE QUIZ:

Before going to a party, look in a full-length mirror.

Are you proud of your outfit? Do you think you
look great? Are you wearing anything made of snakeskin? Do you like your shoes? Do you love them? How
about your hair? Does it exude just the right amount
of glow? Do you adore your haircut? Do your clothes
cost a million dollars? Are they recognizable by designer? Are you free from stains and random wrinkles?

Do you think you look just wonderful?

Consider this: no normal, nonfabulous man on his
way to a party ever thinks he looks even *passable*. His
shoes are dumb, his shirt sports a pale yet glaring beige
stain, his hair is just awful, that's all, awful. A normal
woman looks into her mirror before a party and realizes
her hips would be more appropriate on a sumo wrestler
and that if her jawline were any softer she would be
a Cabbage Patch doll.

If you think you look great when on your way to a
party, you're on the hideous road to becoming a fabulousness fascist.

WHAT IS A FABULOUSNESS FASCIST?

The world is riddled with villains. They stab you in
the knees and demand your wallet. They entice your
children to make porno movies. Real perverts. But
equally horrible in their way are the fabulousness fascists.

And if you look, you can see them everywhere.

They are more prevalent than Presbyterians, more irritating than cheerleaders. They swarm like cockroaches through Manhattan, sucking down gimlets at Mortimer's before raiding Madison Avenue. They riddle Los Angeles, being paged at the Polo Lounge or cadging an invite to Swifty Lazar's Oscar party. They flash emeralds in Dallas, consume Dom Perignon in Des Moines, show off sable in Schenectady.

When people get a certain amount of money, success, or fame, it triggers the latent desire for fabulousness first experienced in the sandbox. If the desire is strong and the brain weak, they enter the fabulousness high-risk category. Smugness sets in, a self-satisfied gleam appears in the eye, and it's curtains.

They will tell you how fabulous everything is. This new band, that new club, some cretinous new hairstyle, some pink nightmare of a new restaurant. Even worse, the fabulousness fascists will tell you who *you* are.

"Why Sally darling! You look fabulous! Puce is *your* color! But darling, you must use *my* hairdresser. Everybody goes to him."

Do not listen to fabulousness fascists. They have no taste. They are sheep dressed in snakeskin. They want what everyone else has, only more and better. A fabulousness fascist will never turn to her mate and say, "What the hell, Harold, let's move to Peru." She can't, because the Peruvians won't notice that her bag is an actual Bottega Veneta, so they won't be consumed by envy, and unless she is surrounded by eyes with green glints in them, a FF isn't sure she exists.

Nobody who's anybody really wants to dedicate her life to fabulousness, since to do so you must give up every spark of originality you ever prided yourself on.

SO OKAY ALREADY! BUT HOW DO I KNOW A FABULOUSNESS FASCIST WHEN I SEE ONE?

He or she will inevitably name-drop, or place-drop, or even thing-drop. As in, "Last week, when we were dining in Mustique with the Princess and Barbara Walters, I dropped my nine-carat emerald in the champagne."

CAN PEOPLE IN SMALL TOWNS WHOM NOBODY WOULD BELIEVE ABOUT BARBARA WALTERS DO THIS?

Sure, as in, "Last week when we were dining at the country club with the mayor and Mrs. Van der Snoot, I dropped my nine-carat emerald in the grits."

I KNOW WHAT YOU MEAN BY A FABULOUSNESS FASCIST. I HATE THEM. HOW CAN I MAKE A FF LOOK SILLY?

You really shouldn't. A FF is the way he is because he is massively insecure and sees the whole world as just a macrocosm of the high-school cafeteria. He is painfully afraid of being ridiculed. So I wouldn't point and laugh at his Gucci buckles. It will only make him sillier.

YOOHOOING AT THE TEA ROOM

Let us picture ourselves in a large restaurant on West Fifty-seventh Street in Manhattan. The tablecloths are pink and the waiters and waitresses are wearing jaunty stage-extra-style Slavic costumes. There is a smallish front room with a coat check, bar, and several minuscule booths. The back room is a huge dining area that still features Christmas decorations, that always features Christmas decorations. There is another floor with another room, but this does not concern us, because this is where they put people from out of town.

This room is called Siberia. We're not there; we're in the socially desirable little booth in the front, eavesdropping.

(Booth one contains an agent and a lazy writer.)

LAZY WRITER· I suppose you think I'm just sitting around all day with my thumb up my ass.

AGENT· I would never accuse you of that form of behavior.

LAZY WRITER· It's just that I'm kind of depressed at the moment. Suicidal, if you must know. Shall I have the chicken kiev? I love the way it squirts. Who is that man over there? God, I wish I could just die. I'm broke.

AGENT· What you must do is write a movie. Speaking of which, there's Lester Famous, Mr. Groovy. The book he just optioned, it's been recalled from the stores. Does he care? He'll make the movie anyway.

LAZY WRITER· Look, there's Sophia.

AGENT· (sotto voce) Poor Sophia. Stop waving! Why wave?

(Booth two contains Sophia, who just lost her job out West, and Faye, who wants to go there. They are in the movie biz.)

FAYE· Why are you waving?

SOPHIA· If Lester can hold his head up, I can too. You think I'm suffering? Ha. I walked out of that place with a year's severance and all my stock.

FAYE· You don't have to pretend to be strong with *me.* I'm your friend. I had nothing to do with it.

SOPHIA· Of course you didn't, darling.

FAYE· Anything I said to them, I said for your own good. I know what you're like, Sophia. You would just work yourself to death if you could. I simply told them we'd discussed it together and decided that I should take over a few of those extra chores.

Sᴏᴘʜɪᴀ• Of course you did, darling. Do you know a good gynecologist?

Fᴀʏᴇ• What's the matter? Oh look, there's Prince Charles's valet.

Sᴏᴘʜɪᴀ• I either have cervical cancer or a yeast infection.

Fᴀʏᴇ• Helen will know, she's riddled with herpes. Yoohoo, Helen! Helen!

(Booth three contains Helen, a studio executive, and Bob, a screenwriter. They are in the movie biz.)

Bᴏʙ• That cow! Don't wave back.

Hᴇʟᴇɴ• How can she eat with her? Doesn't she know? That woman stepped on her face!

Bᴏʙ• Oh, Sophia will be fine. She walked away with six months severance and half her stock. She would like, of course, to think her life is a wreck. There's Lester; poor Lester.

Hᴇʟᴇɴ• Listen, we've decided you must make your characters younger.

Bᴏʙ• Give me a fucking break. I've written in a teenage daughter.

Hᴇʟᴇɴ• What they want, and I have nothing to do with this, is another *Animal House.*

Bᴏʙ• But what we discussed was a hard-hitting Cassavetes-type comedy of manners, with a touch of Neil Simon. People with lines around their eyes. *Annie Hall* of the eighties.

Hᴇʟᴇɴ• And you must realize we need a more upbeat ending. Oh, there's Lazy Writer over there. Do you know her? I should say hello, we put a bid on her book.

Bᴏʙ• Her book was filth. It had no plot. What do

you mean, a new ending? I sweated bullets over that ending.

HELEN· We'll fix it. We'll fix everything. Yoohoo! Lazy Writer!

(Back to booth one:)

LAZY WRITER· Quick, what's her name?

AGENT· Please. She was your best friend two months ago.

LAZY WRITER· She bid nothing on my book. It was an insult.

AGENT· Yoohoo! Harry! Did you like the screening? All your clients up there on the screen! Terrible movie, terrible. You're a brave man, Harry. A good man. I would have shot myself in the foot. *(Turns back to Lazy Writer.)* The manager. You have to be nice to the manager.

LAZY WRITER· You do? Why?

AGENT· Shouldn't you be nice to everyone? I mean, isn't that what it's all about?

NIGHTCLUBS: WHY? HOW?

There are certain people who do not go to nightclubs in search of fabulousness but because nightclubs are what they live for. Garden-variety fabulousness seekers never quite get it right at these glittering yet sleazy night palaces—they either arrive in the wrong model limo or someone in their group is wearing white loafers. They are laughed at and snubbed by bona-fide nightclubsters, who know that to be an integral part of the night scene you must ignore every other aspect of existence, including daytime.

Are you a clubster? Take this quiz and find out.

Do you:

Have a pale gray complexion, a weak grip, and a runny nose?

Intimately know the doorperson of every club in your metropolitan area?

Collapse into a drug- and alcohol-induced coma every Sunday night, from which you finally emerge— red-eyed, foul-breathed, and surly—on Tuesday afternoon?

Go out again on Tuesday evening?

Know who has the drugs, who has the baby laxative, and why?

If you answered yes to many of the above questions, you are a full-fledged bona-fide clubster and needn't read on. But if you're only incipient, and your great wish is to make a splash on the club scene if only you could get a fist in the door, read these instructions with zeal and dedication. It's exacting, arduous work, mastering club scene etiquette, not for those who feel queasy at the sight of spandex.

GETTING READY

Force yourself to sleep until 6 P.M. Then wake up and have breakfast consisting of steak, eggs, salad, fresh raspberries, possibly a split of champagne, and all the known B vitamins. You will not be eating again today.

Then immediately start getting your outfit together. You only have about five hours: not much time. Go to your closet; remove everything black. Rummage through your dirty laundry; remove everything black. If there is a shop in your immediate area, run out, buy something black, and hurry home. Then put all the black items in a neat pile in front of your full-length mirror (for club people, a full-length mirror is tax deductible). Try on every black thing with every other black thing until a certain incredibleness is achieved. You'll know you've hit maximum incredibleness if you look in the mirror and don't know who you are: Are you Mick Jagger? Tina Turner? A Greek shipping magnate? A shopping bag lady? A witness to a hanging?

More than anything, however, you'll look like a sexually appetizing ax murderer. A few leather straps tied judiciously around wrists, ankles, or neck (but never head) may be just the ticket. Eschew anything metallic. Avoid leather railroad caps.

In fact, watch your accessories like a hawk, or they will destroy you. Adorable little bangle bracelets, fun streaks of purple in the hair, amusing brooches and/ or audacious scarves arranged about your person will guarantee you the hairy eyeball. When in doubt, feed it to the dog.

After you're achieved a certain notoriety, you can branch out into colors and do hilarious things with a scarf, but these are subtleties you should not yet attempt. Door people are sharp—they can tell Betsey Johnson from The Gap at a hundred paces. *You* may think you look like a rock guitarist, but they'll decide you're simply a math teacher trying to be weird.

WHERE TO GO AND HOW TO GET IN

I can tell you where to go *now;* that's easy. But I haven't finished writing this book yet. And then it has to be typeset, and then I have to have a fit when I see what the copy editor has done to it. And then the copy editor has to tell me she never understood why I thought I was literate in the first place. Then the book must be printed, bound, and distributed, not to mention how long it will take this book to wend its way to the church rummage sale where you will have bought it. All this takes many years. The half-life of a nightclub is two weeks. So I have no idea where you should go. But I do know one thing: When you go there, you won't get in.

You're not supposed to; it's the law. Going to a nightclub where they don't know who you are is an exercise in self-humiliation. The doormen oblige all pain- and degradation-seekers by making you stand there at the obligatory ropes for hours until you look and feel like a bassett hound who has just had an accident on the Aubusson. And it is not at all uncommon for your fellow rejectees to turn ugly at a moment's notice. I know a girl who had her hand stepped on, her skirt tied around her ankles and half her eyelashes removed when an almost imperceptible gap in the rope dividing the haves and have-nots opened up and the crowd ran amok, doing a sprightly impression of longhorn cattle stampeding to a waterhole.

Nightclub owners love this. They cackle with glee when they peek out at giant hordes of miserable bastards desperately trying to bribe the doormen with hundred-dollar bills or offering their firstborn for sacrifice. "This will get my club into Liz Smith's column for sure," the club owner muses happily, "which will increase business, which will enable me to buy my wife her own Learjet."

In fact, nightclub owners have come up with a new wrinkle: They send out thousands of invitations that say "Big party! Come down to the club! This invitation admits two!" And many a sucker will grab his invite and trot down to the club, only to be asked if he is "on the list."

"Well, no," the sucker says. "List? What list? I have this invitation. It admits two. Here, have a look."

"Very nice," says the doorman, casting a cursory glance, "but are you on the list?"

"I don't understand this list business," the sucker replies. "I get this invitation, the gist of which is to come on down. So I come on down, and here I am. Now let me in."

"You're not on the list, you silly person. Now go away."

If you're not on the list, here's what you do:

Wait until someone gets out of a limo; make sure it's a movie star or a dress designer. As the crowd parts for him/her, attach yourself to the end of his/her entourage. Listen and watch carefully. All the entourage members will kiss the doorman on the cheek and call him by his name, to prove they know what's what. His name may well be Randy.

When Randy confronts you as the interloper you are, kiss him on the cheek. Say, "Hey Randy, I haven't seen you since the *Vampire Lesbians of Sodom* party. What's up? How's your screenplay coming? Anyone here tonight? I'm utterly bored with life. Maybe I should go home, what do you think?"

This should do it. If it doesn't, go back home and change your outfit.

CLIMBING THE LADDER

Once inside mecca, stay away from any dance floors. One must expend energy only in cadging drinks and looking surly, irritated, or bored.

Also stay away from any spacious, well-appointed areas. Nobody worth knowing will be in residence. What you must do is find the V.I.P. room.

Yes! Another citadel to conquer! Your confirmed clubbie will never be caught anywhere *but* the V.I.P. area; he breaks out in pimples at the very notion.

How to spot the V.I.P. area: it's hot, it's crowded, there are hardly any seats, the bar is inaccessible and, if you live in New York City, Sylvia Miles will be there. Sylvia Miles is an actress who achieved fame as a loud-mouthed jezebel in *Midnight Cowboy*. Her goal in life is to go to as many parties as is humanly possible. People have said that Sylvia would attend the opening of an envelope. This is not true. There are no V.I.P. areas or free drink tickets involved in envelope openings.

How to get into the V.I.P. area: just go in. If anyone

tries to stop you, pretend you're Robert de Niro in the "are you talking to me?" scene of *Taxi Driver,* only make your look colder and slightly more homicidal. Make sure not to get your movie roles mixed up so that you start exclaiming, "What's a mook?"

If you want every clubster to be your best friend right away and cover you with kisses the moment you walk through the door, make it a practice to bring every drug known to man with you every time you go out. You will be supremely popular.

But also very poor. And you'll never know if you are loved for yourself and your wonderful high cheekbones or for your Peruvian flake. Instead, develop a scintillating personality. Here's what you should talk about:

How much sleep you haven't been getting.

How the doormen could have let that awful fat girl in.

Who has cab fare to get to the next nightclub.

Whether the next place is really cool or is only pretending to be.

But don't talk about politics. Don't discuss the job interview you had that morning. Don't wonder aloud about the economy. Don't profess your love for New Hampshire. Don't ask whether someone is a man or a woman.

Above all, don't get excited.

WORDS TO AVOID

Before the trouble started, Cleo was a high-spirited, bouncy sort of a girl, energetically pulling her reconditioned Electrolux around her apartment, a do-rag tied to her head, caroling "Diamonds Are a Girl's Best Friend"; or rushing to the airport with all her pretty dresses crammed into a duffel bag to get the last seat on a plane to Memphis to cover the trial of a mother who slayed three; or ringing me up at two in the morning, wondering if I was sleepy or would I like to go out for a drink.

But then some grisly change befell our Cleo. She stopped effervescing and started sulking. I ran into her at a dinner party where she went to sleep on the couch as soon as the meal was over—most disquieting. Then she stopped answering the telephone—very weird.

And then she failed to show up at the most important shoe sale of the year, sparking rumors that she was probably dead.

A BAD LOVE AFFAIR?

A SEVERE FINANCIAL SETBACK?

A CAREER CRISIS?

AN UNPRECEDENTED WEIGHT GAIN?

"Cleo, you must tell me what's wrong!" I said, hammering at her door. She let me in. She finally spoke.

"There I was," she said, "minding my own business. I think I was vacuuming my apartment. I switched on the television. It was on MTV."

"No!" I cried.

"Horrible stuff, I agree," she said. "One of the vee-jays, as I believe they're called, was grinning straight into my face. He spoke.

"He mentioned that it was the end of his shift, that he couldn't wait to go home and 'party.' And he felt that since it was approaching Saturday night, all his viewers would be about ready to 'party down' themselves. In fact, he hoped everyone all across this great nation shortly would be partying their brains out.

"And that's it," she said. "I feel that if people are going to run around saying things like that on national TV, why bother to live?"

"Let's see if I've got this right, Cleo. The word *party* causes you grave despondency?"

"I don't *want* to party," she said. "I especially don't want to party down. And most particularly, if anyone else wants to party or party down, I want them to keep it to themselves."

"It has a slightly collegiate ring to it, to be sure, but..."

"*Party*," Cleo continued, "as far as I am concerned, may never, ever be a verb. One may *go* to a party. One may certainly discover, at a festive event, a partylike atmosphere. And there are, without a doubt, political parties, as well as parties of the first or second part. But!" She punched a pillow. "To use *party* as a verb is an absolute harbinger of the decline and fall of Western civilization, not to mention the end of the world as we know it."

"Oh, surely not," I said.

"Now here, look at this," Cleo said, pulling a heavy volume from her bookshelf. "*Roget's Thesaurus.* A rollicking, free-spirited tome if ever there was one, it has dozens of synonyms for *party*—*fiesta, jamboree, blowout, spree, fling, bender, bust, tear, randan, beanfest, beano, Dewali [Hind.],* and *Bariram [Moham.],* to name but a few. But—and here's the nub—always as a noun. You find no verbs here. Even that cutup of a book will turn up its nose and refuse to speak of verbs."

"I'm beginning to catch your drift," I said. "A loss of standards, you feel, is the beginning of the end. A person who uses *party* as a verb is a person who will walk into a shop and walk out wearing a rubber jumpsuit. Stands to reason."

"Exactly," she said, pouring each of us a shot of tequila. "A person who uses *party* as a verb is a person who, the day after she becomes engaged, will order matches sporting the names Barry and Judy."

"Which would only be amusing should their names happen to be Trevor and Phyllis."

"A person who uses *party* as a verb will also freely use the words *life-style, fabulous,* and *aerobics*," Cleo said.

"Death to those who use *boogie down!*" I said, getting into it. "Instant prefrontal lobotomies for those who feel perfectly justified in peppering their conversations with *awesome!*"

"Using *party* as a verb simply opens the floodgates," she said. "People will start thinking it's okay to talk about being centered, or strung out. They'll offer you a drink by entreating you to name your poison. They'll wonder if it's hot enough for you. These are the same people who snort nose candy and Peruvian marching powder."

"So you feel these are perilous times?"

"A person who uses *party* as a verb will pick up a girl at a disco and tell her that as far as he's concerned, heavy metal music is the finest art form ever produced by humanity. He will then offer the poor bimbo a *freeze* and a lift home in his limo. He will tell her he's never met anyone like her before, and ask her to brunch."

"Brunch! We hate brunch! A blot on humanity's escutcheon."

"At brunch, he will explain in minute detail how his therapy is going, and then suggest a fun jog around the reservoir, followed by Perrier at Zabar's. He will take her out to dinner every night for the following two weeks and will invariably order pasta."

"And arugula salad."

"And then on the fifteenth night he will fail to turn up, then phone her three weeks later and explain that he's afraid of commitment."

"Cleo," I suddenly wondered, "are we speaking autobiographically here? Is a man the subtext of all this?"

"Of course not," she said. "Let's have another drink."

SPIRIT GUIDE

"You Americans are so bloody competitive," the Kiwi has been known to say when we're sitting around with nothing to do and he wants to start trouble. The Kiwi is living with me and is a foreigner. Sometimes he likes to bring a whole group of kiwis to the house for Yank-bashing.

"You Americans are all so bloody *fond* of spectacles," they'll say. "You *worship* winning. You're all gung-ho, mom's apple pie, go-get-'em."

This is my cue to go all squirmily *mea culpa*. If one of the foreigners is a graduate of est training, he may even go so far as to accuse me of being singularly responsible for the entire gamut of American history— it was *me* on that grassy knoll, et cetera.

But, irritatingly enough, they are occasionally on to something. I often become deeply ashamed of the way Americans do try to glorify this sporty business.

The cult of the body motif, although incipiently fascistic, is relatively harmless. But celebrating competition isn't.

"I just love the competitive spirit," chirped a particularly rancid TV sports commentator from my television recently. She had deep reverence in her voice. The other commentators who clustered around her knew just how she felt. They all nodded sagely. No one said, "Oh, put a sock in it, Gladys."

And why not? What's so great about the competitive spirit? Why these worshipful tendencies?

Some things for which the competitive spirit is responsible:

• Women in pinstriped suits with A-line skirts, and running shoes.

- My sister "accidentally" spilling pink nail polish into the works of my brand-new record player when she was seven.
- The specter of thermonuclear war.
- Fabulousness.

I am not advocating the total annihilation of any and all competition. There are times when we simply must push the other guy's face in and stomp on his entrails. But let's not be proud of it. It is in appallingly bad taste to hop around, shriek and whoop, hug everyone in sight and let tears of ecstasy course down one's face simply because one has made another fellow look silly.

From now on, let's be sheepish and weird and ashamed and furtive next time we slime into a taxi in front of a little old lady with a white cane; let's at least *pretend* to be surprised and humble when we win a marathon.

I propose we give the competitive spirit a well-earned rest, and I have come up with a few substitute spirits that are clamoring to be celebrated.

THE SPIRIT OF EXCESS

Let us now praise the man who, just for fun, eats ten jalapeños in a row. Ditto the girl who, on a whim, takes all her money out of the bank to fly to Morocco for the weekend. Medals for anyone who can stay up all night playing poker and smoking cigarettes, then go on to entertain her mother-in-law at a proper ladies' lunch and then not forget to attend a lecture on microbiology.

THE STYLISH SPIRIT

A prime-time all-network awards ceremony honoring those men who have resolutely overcome the urge to pull up the collar and push up the sleeves of their

sports jackets. Also included: women who have eschewed headbands, children who have never sported
a CIAO! backpack, fashion designers who remember
that some women are a chunky five foot two, pimply
youths who refrain from mohawk hairdos, and anyone
who can wear a seersucker suit with aplomb.

THE SPIRIT OF FUTILITY

Kudos to all virgins waiting for their wedding nights.
Hats off to poets who have never considered taking a
meeting with a Hollywood producer, librarians who
try to convince children to read *Lord Jim*, those who
become ballerinas at age thirty-five, anyone still pining
for Eugene McCarthy.

THE NEW YORK SPIRIT

The key to the city to citizens who have climbed from
the bowels of the Broadway-Lafayette subway station
without pausing for a breather. A salute to everyone
who stays in town through August, who knows where
his landlord lives, who has managed to avoid eating
at Blimpie's, who can successfully hail a taxi at Forty-
ninth and Fifth at 4:37 P.M., who has made all the
lights driving down Seventh Avenue, or who can get
a Chinese waiter to smile and say, "On the house."

THE SPIRIT OF GIVING

Eternal approbation to all children who know how to
fix their parents a surefire hangover cure. Honorary
mention to all men who give their loved ones emerald
earrings, to women who don't care that the toilet seat
is left up, to actresses who tell other actresses about
auditions, to supermarket cashiers who take out-of-
date coupons, and to foreign gentlemen who never
utter a surly word about this lovely country.

WHAT IS A YUPPIE?

The most macabre manifestation of fabulousness is the advent of the yuppies. Once merely a gleam in an advertising copywriter's eye, the yuppie is now an established sociological phenomenon, one that threatens to turn the entire fabric of American society into a tattered old rag. (100% Egyptian cotton rag.)

Even as I write this, I can feel the relentless grip of yuppie tentacles insinuating themselves into my brain. You don't know me, but I am a wild girl and have been known to do anything for a laugh. I have consorted with criminally insane rock-and-roll musicians. I have passed out in my dinner—chicken tetrazzini, they tell me it was—through injudicious use of drugs. I have refused to attend college, church, and dental appointments. I have an antiauthoritarian streak that some of the finest minds in the country have called pathological.

And yet I am sitting here writing this in a linen dress. At this point, an incredibly wrinkled linen dress, but still a natural fabric, since I would die before letting a synthetic fiber touch my body. I am even suspicious of silk; I feel it is a cliché. My body emits just the vaguest scent of some classy English soap.

And there has been many a Sunday when I have spent the afternoon going through the *New York Times* real estate section armed with a felt-tipped pen, browsing idly for a co-op or condominium I can afford. This is unsavory enough. Even worse is that one of the neighborhoods I have my eye on is festooned with banners that read, Stop Gentrification.

Plus I know all about extravirgin olive oil and aged balsamic vinegar, and am not surprised to find both anointing my salad. It's true that I have not gone so far as to actually buy these items, but I suspect that even being vaguely aware of their existence is damning. Listen, I even know that pesto is passé.

The worst, however, is my garment-bag quest, which rivals the hunt for the Holy Grail in its intensity. I used to use an old garment bag left behind by some boyfriend, which worked fine even though he bought it on the street for four dollars. But when it burst open on the way down the baggage chute at Kennedy Airport, exposing plenty of suspect silk lingerie to the hilarity of my fellow passengers, I realized it was time for new luggage.

What a production. First of all, I won't have a garment bag emblazoned with any brand name, no matter how fancy. Even Pierre Cardin. Especially Pierre Cardin. This is neither here nor there, but is Pierre Cardin a real person? Does he still exist? Have you noticed that there's a Pierre Cardin everything? Even telephones?

Then I realized it wouldn't do to have anything vinyl. At one point I found a great garment bag with just the right amount of leather trim. I was all set to buy it, but then I noticed that the seams were piped with a substance that was merely *pretending* to be leather. A dreadful moment.

Vinyl nowadays manages to look and feel exactly like leather. I get all crazed and try to stick the stuff up my nose, in hopes of detecting a telltale cowhide whiff. No trim at all is a hundred times better than alleged leather. And I don't want nylon, I want canvas.

You can understand my horror. I don't *want* to be a yuppie. Remember when the term *yuppie* surfaced? It was, I believe, during the 1984 Presidential campaign, when the media didn't know what to call those business-suited, running-shoed clones who were so hot on Senator Gary Hart. Young upwardly mobile professional: *yuppie*. A fun term. It caught on. Big. A new subculture was created. Now we all know what to call those rowdy and arrogant business-suited parties who clog Manhattan restaurants and humiliate waitresses. Now people who like balsamic vinegar but otherwise don't know who they are know how to define themselves.

But as we know, when someone smacks a label on us, we tend to act accordingly. I'm petrified that one morning I'm going to wake up and want brunch. And that soon afterward I will find myself in some horribly spacious, blond-wooded restaurant riddled with ferns and pale flowers, sipping precious mineral water and munching on goat cheese fritters. And that I'll be *happy*.

Please lord no, anything else. Yuppies have no soul.

A yuppie is nothing but a preppie with a gay sensibility. Consider where we first saw those hallmarks of yuppiedom: art deco, pale pink napkins, designer gym outfits. But yuppies are not gay; that would be too exciting and flamboyant. Yuppies simply want *things*.

Things make yuppies feel better, more secure. Who cares about nuclear proliferation if we've just bought a new Cuisinart attachment? And isn't shopping a lot safer than Valium? Possessions, for the terminally frightened, bring peace of mind.

And, mired here in the eighties, we need all the peace we can get. The country is suffering from musical-chairs syndrome. We all dance around for a bit and then when we try to sit down again, somebody doesn't have a chair. We're running scared; we want *ours*. The haves and have-nots are more defined than ever. Yuppies are young and strong and will grab any chair they can get.

Ethics are the province of the bleeding-heart types, stale relics from the sixties who care about the poor, who feel a brotherhood with the disenfranchised. How can yuppies possibly care about the poor? They wear polyester. And tacky designer jeans! They don't have interesting careers!

So what if there's a luncheonette attached to a building that a yuppie wants to buy? So what if the luncheonette owner has been there for forty years, selling milkshakes and egg creams, dispensing gossip, and keeping an eye on the neighborhood kids? If a yuppie can get three times the rent from a florist who flies in tulips every day from Holland and charges eight dollars a stem, he's going to kick that low-rent old luncheonette owner into the gutter. When a neighborhood is going upscale, it's every yuppie for himself.

And the florist selling those eight-dollar tulips will soon have a very nice house in the Hamptons, because a yuppie is only happy when he's paying too much for something. Your yuppie doesn't want some boring old maple syrup from Nowhere, New Jersey. He wants that ever-so-precious, ever-so-amber maple syrup from that special tree in that ineffably quaint town in Vermont. So much more attractively packaged.

When yuppies get hold of a trend, it's curtains. Remember a few years ago when they decided that Cajun food was hip? How two hundred Cajun joints opened during a single weekend, selling dirty rice at humorous prices?

Not that they'll start trends. You can't if you're boring and conservative and slavishly concerned with status. They are a trend in themselves, an unpleasant amalgam of the seventies and eighties: self-involved, economically conservative.

My wrinkled linen dress is simply drenched with moral indignation! How dare these people live in my world, clutter up space in my brain? Bring back eccentrics, I say.

Would a yuppie ever act crazy? Would a yuppie go off into the night with a mysterious stranger? Would a yuppie hang a pair of fuzzy dice from his rearview mirror?

The weirdest thing a yuppie ever does is get herpes. This is not weird enough. We must all be very vigilant and not let them take over the world.

You first; I have to go shopping.

MICHAEL JACKSON'S NOSE JOB

Not only are award ceremonies the most explicit manifestation of fabulousness, they are also a capitalistic plot to keep us all in our places, especially if it's something like IBM awarding its secretaries. But I don't care. If there's an award ceremony on prime-time TV, I'm right there, my eyes glued to the set. And my friends are there with me, since the real purpose of these extravaganzas is to dish everyone and everything. What other fun do we have these days? Everyone is either brokenhearted, penniless, or both. There was a jolly gathering just the other night.

Lucy (best marathon shopper) made the chili and invited only people she knew would become vicious at a moment's notice if she poured enough wine down their throats. Everyone immediately started jockeying for position around the TV, with Jake (best eyebrow raiser) scoring the most central and comfortable armchair.

"Cynthia (best slug) usually drapes herself across the entire sofa. She's being very well behaved tonight," Lucy said. I wedged myself between the Kiwi (best dinner eater) and Herb (best fake French accent).

A pool was organized by Brodie (best child who ever lived) and Neville (best John Cleese imitation). Everybody would guess the winners, then put five dollars into the hat, winner take all. This was pretty exciting, since we all knew we'd win. We were all eager to begin, except Cleo (best polyester detector), who, terrified that someone would use *party* incorrectly, fell asleep in her chair.

Ann Reinking was our first victim.

"Oh, I love her," Lucy said.

"No you don't," said Herb. "You're just English. We'll have to begin your American show-biz indoctrination immediately. Watch Ann, she's had more lessons than the astronauts." Rita (best whistler through teeth) became enamored of Herb at that very moment, which was fascinating. Would Rita, a six-foot-tall red-headed smart-aleck girl from Texas, find happiness with Herb, a six-foot-tall semi-reclusive blindingly cynical actor from New York?

"Why are they clapping just because she got lifted into the air?" Brodie wondered.

"They haven't seen anybody lifted in Los Angeles for ages," Herb said. "Nobody out there does anything for anybody."

"It's so clear that her teeth have been capped," Lucy said, proving to be a quick learner.

Glenn Close elicited shrieks. "What's wrong with her?" Rita wondered. "She looks like she's posing for a fifty-cent piece."

"It's the hairdo," said Cleo, suddenly snapping awake. "The dress, but mainly the hairdo. She's been using Margaret Dumont's hairdresser."

Prince! We were completely entranced! A spangled snood and also that mustache! What is the purpose of that upper-lip foliage?

"And most of all, I'd like to thank God," Prince said.

"Who lent me this robe," Jake added.

Things we decided we would say if Prince ever happened to drop in:

"Drop your cowl anywhere."

"Make merry with my setting gel."

"Help yourself to any rhinestones around the house."

"I hate a God-botherer," Lucy decided.

"He's only copying Michael Jackson," Brodie said.

"I guess this is the atheist awards party," Herb said.

"Did God tell Michael Jackson to get a nose job?" Rita wondered. "If so, it was a mistake. I liked the old, fatter nose. Kind of sexy. Like Herb's."

"I never like the way Michael Jackson plucks his eyebrows," pondered Lucy, "and I've never been really partial to eye shadow and blusher on a man."

"That's because you're old and boring and uncool," said Brodie, a recent frequenter of the *Rocky Horror Picture Show.* "The only thing wrong with Michael Jackson besides the nose job is that he talks exactly like Mickey Mouse."

"And he's always telling us how deeply moved he is," said the Kiwi. "Look at Diana Ross's earrings! Fulsome, don't we think?"

"Oh my God, I'm so excited," I said.

"Why? Because your boyfriend has finally learned how to accessory-dish?" asked Lucy.

"No, because he is at last becoming earring-conscious. She's still angling for those emeralds," Rita said.

Cleo awoke and realized with horror that she had been sleeping with her mouth open, and that there was a slight amount of drool involved. "Could somebody please put a cloth over my cage?" she muttered.

Stevie Wonder also spangled!

JAKE· Don't you wonder if they lie to him about his outfits? "Oh, no, Stevie, of *course* you're not wearing sequins."

STEVIE· I'd like to share this with you...

LUCY· Don't share, Stevie, don't share.

RITA· Cynthia, take your finger out of your nose.

NEVILLE· I saw a porno film the other day called *Romancing the Bone.*

Sally Field's hairdo was also disconcerting and probably directly responsible for her hysteria.

"You like me, you like me!" Sally screamed.

"Sally, take a Valium," Cleo commanded.

"The audience should yell back, 'No, *we hate you.* But we liked your acting,'" Herb said.

Brodie, being fifteen, won the pool with a perfect score. A fifteen-year-old, I have discovered, is the perfect embodiment of mass mind. He has not yet acquired any eccentricities of taste; he is simply a manifestation of the crudest and most commercial level of the collective unconscious. If a fifteen-year-old loves your song, it will go platinum. Any movie he's fervent about is bound to break box-office records. All smart producers have fifteen-year-olds on the payroll.

"Thank you one and all," said Brodie, receiving his winnings. "I would especially like to thank my mom for having me, so that I could be here with you now. I will take this money and buy several albums and a Prince poster. You have all been very kind. I know I speak for my mom as well when I invite you all over next month to watch the Grammy awards. Another opportunity to be evil without hurting anyone."

LIFE-STYLES OF THE POOR AND OBSCURE

I have been waiting around for that unctuous person for months now. You know the variety of human blot of which I speak—one of those peculiar grinning types who narrate television shows about the rich and famous, who oil their way into celebrity homes so that we, the television audience, can satiate our desires to find out *just exactly* how much Joan Collins's breakfast nook cost. We can also—if we haven't nipped down-

stairs to pay the Chinese restaurant delivery guy—get
a gander at George Harrison's toilet. Or discover Jill
St. John's most intimate feelings as she pulls a moody
weed from her sumptuous garden.

People have told me that these shows featuring celebrity purchases only last one hour, but I know they're
kidding. I have felt the seasons change while watching
one. During another my son progressed from chewing
on zwieback to demanding the car keys. Occasionally
my gorge overflows and I make forays from my sofa
to dismantle the television, only to have my hand
slapped away by one or another of my significant
others, who simply has to know about Debbie Reynolds's mink coat.

I understand this fascination with Debbie Reynolds's
mink coat completely. I feel it every day when I read
the *Daily News: 11-YEAR-OLD SHOT BY TERRORISTS!
EARTHQUAKE KILLS 50,000! TODDLER PERISHES IN TEN-
EMENT FIRE WHILE TRYING TO SAVE INFANT SISTER!
HEADLESS BODY FOUND IN TOPLESS BAR!*

Then I turn the page and, suddenly, Debbie Reynolds's mink coat! Thank God! Debbie, strut your
stuff! I want to know all! Erase from my mind those
fifty-thousand earthquake victims, and make it quick!

I will get much mileage out of Debbie and her coat.
I will be able to take tales of it to the cocktail party
tonight, where I will meet perfect strangers of whom
I know nothing and with whom I can discuss Debbie's
fur quite happily. If we lived in a small town, we would
discuss how the doctor was putting his leg over the
mayor's wife, but in big cities we discuss Debbie. Movie
stars have taken the place of community elders.

"Actually, it was Henry Fonda who killed Sal
Mineo," I can say to everyone, and they'll be riveted.

Pretty soon, I think, people will be discussing *me*
at cocktail parties. The way I figure it, what with the
lengthiness of these celebrity shows and the amount
of celebrity pages in all newspapers and magazines,

they are going to run out of bona-fide rich and famous persons pretty damned fast. How many soap opera actors with live-in blond girlfriends who are gourmet sushi cooks can there be? Only a few hundred thousand, certainly, and when they use all of them up they're going to have to descend, and then descend some more, and then even some more. And it is only a small step from the barely rich and hardly famous to the vaguely solvent and somewhat mobile—in other words, *moi*.

Any day now a fruity-voiced entity is going to ring my doorbell, and I'll be ready. I have prepared tasteful answers to his inevitable questions. Here is a preview of what you will be seeing on prime-time television in the near future:

OILY PERSON· Cynthia, why did you tell me to meet you in this thrift shop?

ME· Ha ha ha. This is my *home*, you silly fellow. Where I create, where I commune with my muse and my nearest and dearest, where I find repose and take sustenance.

OILY PERSON· Ah, of course. Tell me of the vast significance of that pile of wet towels on that chair.

ME· I like to leave them there. There's something about a towel rack that is so *bourgeois* and *predictable*, don't you think? But here, perhaps you'd like to sit down. No, no, I wouldn't even attempt that sofa. The dog committed a small indiscretion last night, you know what Labrador retrievers are. Take the chair. I'll just dump these towels in the kitchen.

OILY PERSON· I see that your piquant sense of humor leads you to do your ironing on the floor.

ME· That and the fact that there is no table. What with one thing and another...

OILY PERSON· That dress you've been ironing. Very unique. How much would you say it cost?

ME· Do you know, if I had bought this dress in September it would have cost $540? But by buying it when it is nearly out of fashion and with a judicious switching of the tags, it was only $35!

OILY PERSON· A canny move. And what will you do with the other $505?

ME· I thought I might put a down payment on a villa just outside Cannes. I have a picture of it somewhere.

OILY PERSON· Perhaps in that luxuriously untidy mountain of papers over there...

ME· That's my next book.

OILY PERSON· Do you write to pass the time? To plumb the ineffable depths of human nature? To purge the dark demons of your soul? To let play your rampant creativity?

ME· All those things. Plus eating. It's adorable how fond one can become of eating.

OILY PERSON· How much money did you make last year?

ME· Ooh la la!

OILY PERSON· Tell our viewers about your glittering social life.

ME· Well, I wake in the early afternoon...

OILY PERSON· Could that be your bed in there?

ME· Yes, only a hop, skip, and a jump away. Most convenient. I do love to live somewhere small and cozy, don't you?

OILY PERSON· Um, ah.

ME· And I find the idea of making a bed so trivial. I wake up and turn to my live-in lover—he makes the most wonderful bean dish, by the way...

OILY PERSON· Where is he at the moment?

ME· Did you happen to pass a man with a saxophone

and an upturned hat on the street, probably next to the dry cleaner?

OILY PERSON· A most attractive young man.

ME· And so talented and industrious. Perhaps you have a vacancy for a saxophonist on your show?

OILY PERSON· He feels the need to express his creativity?

ME· Don't we all?

OILY PERSON· What's that peculiar contraption in the corner?

ME· That is my teenage son.

OILY PERSON· Home from boarding school?

ME· That would explain it.

OILY PERSON· Tell me about your glittering social life.

ME· Not much to tell, really...

OUTFITS

WE ARE NOT WHAT WE WEAR

Want to be cool, with it, up-to-date fashionable, on the cutting edge? Want to have drop-dead clothes, a chic look, an impeccable image?

Sorry. Can't be done. It is no longer fashionable to be fashionable. The more we try, the more we are destined for failure. We will be met with scorn and branded old hat, gauche, and bad form. If we're trendy, we're twits, and no one will want to chat with us at the Laundromat.

Here's why.

Back in the old days, when artists used to live in lofts, if one had a "look," it meant something. Some looks proclaimed, "Hi there, I'm a rock star!" or "Hello, I'm a black humorist!" or even "Yo! I'm a drug dealer!"

This made things easy. If you, an artist, were walking down the street (wearing, possibly, black tights and paint-spattered multicolored rags), and coming toward you was another vision in black tights et cetera, you could say to yourself, "There's another artist coming toward me," and you'd be right. You would then be reminded that you were a member of a peer group, which would put a jaunty spring in your step.

But now dentists and people with hyphenated names live in lofts in places like Soho (New York) and downtown L.A., and hundreds of thousands of square feet— once places where people in multicolored rags would peer with intense dislike at canvases, then grab a tube of vermilion, squish it around on the palette, rush at the canvas and make a few decisive dabs, view their handiwork, and go all mournful again—are used to showcase the perfect bit of deco, a museum-quality collection of Stickley armchairs, or the *dernier cri* in Memphis furniture.

Lofts are no longer arenas in which to be incessantly creative. Dentists and people with hyphenated names have made them into status symbols and are wearing multicolored rags, and nothing is what it seems.

Here's what else we can't wear:

ROCK-STAR REGALIA Even rock stars wouldn't be caught dead in studded leather, a cross dangling from one ear and a bandanna tied around the biceps. Neither would they think of appearing in brocade velvet and ruffled shirts with impeccable makeup and their hair tied back in a ponytail. They know too well that in either case people will just mistake them for hairdressers.

THE MENTAL JAPANESE LOOK Everyone knows these strange and baggy clothes are not worn by actual Japanese people—how would they afford it?—but by rich, bored housewives from possibly the Upper East Side of Manhattan whose husbands are fooling around and feeling guilty. Some salesgirls don these outfits as a joke.

THE ARMY-SURPLUS EFFECT These threads are never worn by war veterans, only by extremely tall models or Aryan Europeans with artistic aspirations and sadomasochistic tendencies.

THE PREPPIE GAG No longer do Lacoste shirts and Topsiders have anything to do with where the wearer went to school or who his family is. These togs are now the province of those who are afraid to wear anything else. Such as agents whose wives are in public relations, *New York Times* reporters, anyone in advertising, or cocaine dealers.

SCI-FI FUTURIST GARB, including jumpsuits with enormously padded shoulders and modified Nehru collars, is not worn by spacemen or astronomers, but instead by persons who say they are video producers. When they actually find time to produce these rock videos is beyond me, since these specimens are invariably found passing joints in deserted corners of rock clubs. Anyone who tells us he's a video producer is simply ashamed to say he's between jobs.

FIFTIES CLOTHING is only worn by children who were not around at the time.

It is conceivable that TWEED JACKETS AND OLD SCHOOL TIES are occasionally worn by Englishmen, but nine out of ten wearers (usually the ones with their collars and sleeves pushed up) are actually men who hang around the bar at fancy frog restaurants where they get drunk and abuse women. They intimate subtly that they are songwriters, or about to start that novel, and when confronted with the accusation that they are helping run daddy's rag trade business, they ooze away.

DESIGNER CLOTHING is worn unceasingly by social climbers. Designer sweat suits are worn by poor social climbers.

RIDING COSTUMES have never been so far removed from those who have ever cleared a hurdle, and are now embraced by those who spent their formative years in the suburbs of Detroit and are afraid people might find out.

ATHLETIC OUTFITS are not worn by athletes, who inexplicably wear designer jeans, but by psychologists and holistic practitioners intent upon striving for excellence.

The POSTNUCLEAR look is shunned by survivors of Hiroshima but adopted by second-class rock musicians who like to watch themselves on TV.

Where does this leave us? With nothing to wear, that's where.

If this were not a democracy, we could force dentists and hairdressers back into their white coats and devise special uniforms for all agents and rock video produc-

ers, but alas, they will have their sartorial freedom
whether the rest of us wish it or not.

In this time of rampant posing, we must with dignity
withdraw from the fray and simply never let our clothing make a statement. It just doesn't have a big enough
vocabulary.

DESIGNS OF THE FUTURE:
A SCIENCE-FICTION STORY

"Hello, Madge! Am I disturbing you?"

"Of course not, Adrianna, I was hoping you'd stop
by before you went shopping. I want you to taste this
new coffee cake. Come right on in."

"Why, Madge, you sly fox! You've bought yourself
some new kitchen chairs! They're simply heaven!"

"Do you like them?" asked Madge, biting her lip
in anxiety. "I'm just not sure about the color of the
seat cushions. And the line of the legs—are they just
a tad stocky, do you think?"

"Nonsense, pet, they're marvelous!" said Adrianna,
running a polished fingernail along the seat back.
"Whose are they?"

"They're Calvin's. You know, I think the man has
gone kitchen-mad. He's making faux marble rolling
pins in twenty-four colors. In fact, that's his coffee
cake you've been munching on with those pearly
Gianni Versace teeth of yours."

"Really? Calvin's making coffee cake? Fascinating."
Adrianna swallowed thoughtfully. "Not bad, really.
Perhaps I should try it on Trevor. Although he pro-
fesses to be my slave when I serve him Missoni flap-
jacks. Last night he positively *showered* me with Ralph
Lauren roses."

"Ralph is making roses? I didn't know that. What
colors?"

"Dusky magenta, creamery yellow, sexually explicit red, shrinking violet, and heroin white," recited Adrianna. "I don't know where the man finds the time. Did you hear he bought Cleveland, Ohio, last Thursday? I can't wait to see how he furnishes it!"

"Lots of paisley, I should imagine; the man's tradition-mad."

"Although you never know, he may go all cowboy and rugged..."

"Or wildly Aztec. Ralph's so capricious. Remember when he only designed clothes?"

"He didn't really! Think of it, only clothes. How did he make ends meet?"

"Sometimes I wish *I* were a designer," said Madge, serving Adrianna another cup of Zhandra Rhodes's Caff-U-Luv. "Sometimes I get so bored with shopping. I was trying to choose a clock radio the other day. So confusing! The Pierre Cardin Snooz-Alert is a nice shade of dove gray, but with maroon trim. Maroon! The Jasper Conran Wake-Up Sucker was just too wildly *large*, the Gaultier Night-and-Daze only comes in an unfortunate puce, and whatever can Norma Kamali be thinking? Her Dream Machine was shaped like a rosebush!"

"It's her English country-chintz look," said Adrianna.

"Yes, of course. But suddenly I just couldn't bear it! There wasn't one clock radio that I liked. I had this vision of myself rampaging through the aisles screaming, 'Just give me something plain and beige with no one's name on it!'"

"Madge, how do you feel? You don't look very well. Feeling feverish? Despondent? Want a Claude Montana Stim-U-Brain?"

"Adrianna, if you must know, I'm pregnant." Madge pressed her hands to her temples.

Adrianna yelped and squealed. "Whose is it, you lucky girl? How much did it cost?"

"Adrianna, it's mine."

"Of course it is, dear, but *whose is it?* Which sperm bank did you go to? Say you didn't go to Sonia Rykiel's—all her babies emerge so angular and sooty-eyed. I know—Armani! The best! Such a good tailor! Those perfect eyelids! Say I'm right!"

"It's mine, Adrianna. Mine and Ralph's."

"Well, sweetheart, that's just sweet. And Ralph makes such precious diapers and nighties that perfectly match the babies' eyes. Which model? The Wild Bill Hickok? The Young Baron? The Vassar Graduate?"

"Not Ralph Lauren. I mean my husband."

"Not Ralph!"

"Yes, Ralph."

"Darling, so careless of you! How did it happen?"

"Oh, in the usual way, Adrianna."

"But darling, you simply must have an abortion, that's all."

"I don't want an abortion! I want a plain beige clock radio!"

"Of course you do, my angel. And I think you need a nice morning rest before your shopping. I have a wonderful, soothing book I could lend you: *War and Peace*, as adapted by Donna Karan. 'A sprightly farce,' *Bill Blass Magazine* called it."

"No thanks."

"There's a documentary on antique pleating methods on the Mary McFadden Network."

"Seen it. It's derivative."

"Oh, Madge!"

"I know, I know. Something's got into me. I'm feeling all sort of restless and Rudi Gernreich. I want to break out! Be wild! I want to do something! I want to conduct the Brandenburg Concerto!"

"Now Madge, you know that Geoffrey Beene has already conducted the Brandenburg."

"They do everything! It's just not fair! I remember when I was just a little girl and my parents were having a fight. My mother had bought an Issey Miyake comforter, and my father was livid. 'Where will it all end, Doris?' he kept screaming. He died soon afterward. My mother kept telling him not to worry, it was just a nice comforter, she didn't even notice it was made by a designer. But he kept screaming that Issey Miyake was some kind of dreadful harbinger."

"But Madge, your father is still alive."

"That's not my father, that's an Alaia Android."

"Ah, well, that explains it."

"Yes, I suppose it does," said Madge heavily. "More Caff-U-Luv?"

CLOTHING DOS AND DON'TS

For that highly specialized and monumentally important topic of dressing yourself, we have been fortunate to persuade Sister Soignée, high priestess of outfits, to answer your questions.

Although she has never curated a textile show at the Metropolitan Museum of Art, Sister Soignée comes to us with impeccable credentials: She was the first girl in Philadelphia to wear a miniskirt with black fishnet stockings; she is the distinguished author of the treatise "Why Anyone Who Likes Orange Is a Dork"; she has never once succumbed to the lure of metallic ankle boots; and she is leading a lobby in Washington that hopes to make headbands worn by either sex a felony.

■

Dear Sister Soignée:

I know that Bloomingdale's is supposed to be a very chic place, but every time I go in there I experience a dreadful anxiety attack. I start to sweat, get a headache, and often find myself sitting on the floor in the lingerie section with no recollection of how I got there.

*On my last visit, I found a gorgeous teal-green
sweater for $27, but I fainted before I could give
the saleswoman my money. Am I insane?*
Natalie

Dear Natalie:

The symptoms you describe indicate that you
have succumbed to a new strain of urban disease.
Scientists call it the B-Hysteric syndrome (BHS),
since it occurs only in expensive department stores
beginning with the letter B. All over Bergdorf's,
Bendel's, Bonwit's, and especially Bloomingdale's, shoppers are suffering.

Count yourself lucky, Natalie; your symptoms
are mild. BHS victims have been known to foam
at the mouth, become wildly abusive and even
violent (assistant buyers have been stabbed), experience uncontrollable itching or sobbing, and
have paranoid delusions.

Only last month one shopper removed dozens
of Nippon dresses from the racks and proceeded
to stomp heavily upon them, insisting to store
security guards that she was Diana Vreeland and
knew precisely what she was doing. (The poor
woman is still heavily sedated and is routinely
restrained from boarding planes to Paris to visit
Sonia Rykiel.)

Experts are baffled, but the latest theories pos-
tulate that this tragic disease has been caused by
department store designers running amok. It
seems that in their zeal to get people to buy, buy,
buy, these store planners have created anxiety-
provoking floor plans. Shoppers are forced to become dizzy running from one counter to another,
looking for bargains so prominently advertised in
their Sunday newspapers. Department store per-
sonnel thought the shoppers would become so
confused they would buy everything in sight, but
their perfidy backfired, tragically.

The cure? Complete abstinence for several months, after which time victims may visit small boutiques. But they should never again venture into department stores unless accompanied by a trained nurse.

Sister Soignée

■

Dear Sister Soignée:

Please tell me why my girlfriend won't let me wear my scarf. My grandmother crocheted it for me, it's brown and gray, and I like it a lot. When I knot it around my throat, it hangs down to my knees, which makes me feel kind of racy and rogue-like, especially when I fling one end over my shoulder.

But my girlfriend gets this terrible look on her face, as if she'd just eaten a crate of lemons. "Wear that and you go to the movies by yourself, Steve," she says. My name is Steve. I don't understand her disdain, and she won't explain. Should I rebel?

Steve

Dear Steve:

The generosity of women never ceases to amaze me. There you are with an eight-foot scarf and your girlfriend sticks by you, even in winter.

If you look very carefully at your scarf, and try to be dispassionate and not think of Grandma, you will begin to discern that such an item was only worn in the mid-seventies, the dark ages of fashion—what we call the macramé era.

Tuck this thing in the back of your drawer immediately. Only let it resurface when visiting Grandma. Scarves on men should be short, sweet, and simple. Never let them make a "statement." They simply cannot cope.

Sister Soignée

■

Dear Sister Soignée:

I go shopping. I see all these big dresses. Some are like huge shirts that droop to mid-calf. Some are like giant sundresses with dropped waists.

I try these dresses on. I immediately turn into a baby hippo. I'm not fat either. Slightly hippy, maybe. An ample bust area, certainly. But nobody would refer to me as "that fat girl." Unless they saw me in one of these mammoth dresses.

So I haven't bought one yet. But everyone else has. Should I?

Rita

Dear Rita:

Don't you have a mother? When you were a teenager and wanted to go to an all-night twist party because your best friend Judy was going, didn't your mother say, "And I suppose if Judy jumped off the Empire State Building, you would too?"

Just because a bunch of frogs who are all arms and legs, six feet tall, and weigh 98 pounds decide to festoon themselves in excessive yardage doesn't mean you have to turn yourself into a walking lampshade.

Fashion is to be used and abused with abandon. Never let it get the upper hand and use *you*. A fashion victim is never a pretty sight.

Sister Soignée

■

Dear Sister Soignée:

Can a person be a rampant left-wing socialist sort of a guy and still wear stylish clothes?

I went to a union meeting the other day wearing a really incredible Katherine Hamnett jumpsuit and consequently nobody would talk to me.

This doesn't seem fair. I like to dress up.

Geoffrey

Dear Geoffrey:

Politicos who look askance at stylish clothing are harboring an unsavory nostalgia for the sixties.

Back then, if you weren't wearing a slightly stained ribbed turtleneck and jeans with lumpy pockets that bagged at the ass, you had no credibility.

Clothes were a political statement during the sixties, which was too bad, since it kept all clothes-horses from attending those tedious committee meetings and endless marches where they would have brightened the proceedings considerably.

Being smart and festive is your God-given right. Except if you're wearing a cashmere blazer with brass buttons and tasseled loafers, in which case you can only expect people to point and laugh.

Sister Soignée

■

Dear Sister Soignée:

Should children be permitted to wear clothing dictated by brand names? My ten-year-old daughter says she will simply die if not permitted to wear a pair of Reeboks, because no one will ever speak to her again.

Mom

Dear Mom:

A child may wear whatever she likes to school, providing her parents can afford it. Sinister and ritualistic mayhem is routine among the young; they have grisly tribal codes that mean nothing to grown-ups. Without her pair of Reeboks as a totem, your daughter may indeed be in jeopardy.

But when your child goes out with you, she constitutes an accessory. Exercise your authority.

Sister Soignée

■

Dear Sister Soignée:

Have you any thoughts on the fur problem? I bought a fur hat recently. I look terrific in it.

"Take that horrible thing off your head immediately," said my boyfriend. "You look like some rich bimbo."

"Mother," said my son, "it's gross to be walking around with a dead animal on your head."

"Wear that thing," said my boyfriend, "and I will not kiss you. I will not so much as hold your hand."

Naturally, there was no way in hell I was going to take my hat off. I flaunted it all evening, keeping it on my head during dinner even though it made my head sweat.

But my heart wasn't in it. The men never stopped their raillery for an instant, and by the end of the night I felt like a leper. And not an attractive leper.

I would like to point out that I am not particularly a fur person. I think that fur coats, jackets, and stoles are ostentatious and impractical. But a hat, I thought, was just the ticket. Breezily insouciant with just a smidgeon of decadence. A touch perverse. Dashing.

What to do?

Rhoda

Dear Rhoda:

Take a tip from Bertie Wooster, P. G. Wodehouses's famed antihero. Here's the scenario:

Poor Bertie will be innocently tucking into his morning kipper while Jeeves unpacks his suitcase when suddenly he (Bertie) discerns a distinct chill in the air. Jeeves has unearthed a white dinner jacket that Bertie has brought back from Cannes. Jeeves cocks an eyebrow, and Bertie, poor sap, knows he is in the soup. He will try mightily to be a man of iron for two hundred pages or so, but by the end of the book we all know that he will be wrapping that white dinner jacket in brown paper and donating it to the deserving poor.

But before this *denouement*, he persuades Jeeves to perform some major service, usually getting him unengaged to a girl who thinks the stars are God's daisy chain.

Yes, we're talking about a little light blackmail here. It's true that you are completely in the soup, since no girl can hold out against both a son and a lover, but brazen it out for a while. Wait until they both want to go mountain climbing and you want to go to Paris. Or when you want to spend the $500 earmarked for a new water heater on a black dress. Then you can say, "Take me to Paris and my hideous fur hat goes out the window."

It always works for Bertie.

Sister Soignée

■

Dear Sister Soignée:

Out of nowhere, I suddenly must have salmon-colored clothes.

I crave salmon shoes, salmon sweaters, salmon coats. I walk down the street, minding my own business, and the next thing I know my eye has been caught by some sort of salmon something in a shop window and then my body is arrested in mid-stride and I am standing there transfixed and open-mouthed in front of a child's salmon pinafore (size 4).

What could this mean? I am an all-black sort of person, a less-is-more Japanese-designer sort of person. I haven't worn a frill since 1969, at age eleven. I don't like salmon. But I want it desperately.

Doris

Dear Doris:

The fashion force is at work again.

As every girl knows, there lurks in the brain not only the medulla oblongata and the cortex, but also the small yet fiercely powerful fashion nodule. Each woman's tiny nodule is linked, possibly through some form of sophisticated extraterrestrial microwave, to every other woman's nodule, thus producing the collective fashion nodule force (CFNF).

The CFNF emits waves that make us all want to appear this year in long straight skirts, that make us suddenly crave Robert Clergerie shoes, that force us to despise everything with a blouson motif.

Just recently it was as if there were a great disturbance in the force, as if many voices cried out "Salmon!" and were then stilled forever.

Follow these voices if you must, but be assured that every time you turn a corner you will meet a variation of yourself.

Sister Soignée

■

Dear Sister Soignée:

What about a down coat? Is this an item too horrible to wear?

Just Wondering

Dear Just:

Down jackets that keep very quiet about themselves are okay. They must never be shiny, and they must make no pert fashion statement. They must be plain, tedious, and efficient.

Down vests with the above attributes are also acceptable. Khaki is the preferred color.

Long down coats on either sex should never emerge from one's closet unless severe storm warnings are in effect—only when television stations keep breaking into their regular programming to focus upon their shivering correspondents freezing in snowdrifts and telling us what the wind-chill factor is now.

Never wear a down coat to a nightclub.

Sister Soignée

■

Dear Sister Soignée:

I've been falling in love with a man for about three months now. A decent fellow, if you like guys with glasses, as I do. So it was getting sort of serious—I had decided to stop seeing other people, gave him the bottom drawer of the bureau— when a disquieting occurrence occurred.

He arrived at the door last night carrying a bouquet of flowers and wearing leather trousers.

Brown leather trousers, all soft and supple with that special expensive leather sheen; must have cost a couple of hundred dollars.

Well, I almost threw up.

I didn't think I had any thoughts about leather trousers. I mean, why would I? I can vaguely recall always looking away whenever a pair of them would swivel before my face, but I'd never delved.

Yet now I've gone off this man completely. The idea of him ripping off my clothes and covering me with steamy kisses causes those waves of nausea to reappear with a vengeance.

Sally

Dear Sally:

All my sympathies. If this happened to me, not that it would, since I have devoted my life to the study of clothes and have no time for steamy kisses, but say for science it ever happened, here's what I would do:

I would slam the door in his face. I would

take two Valiums and go to sleep. I might contemplate packing my bags and moving to India, where I hear it is a capital offense to wear leather.

Although leather shoes and belts are perfectly acceptable, leather jackets quite sexy on some, and leather miniskirts adorable on teenagers, leather trousers are a blot.

A human wearing leather trousers is a human who would call the waiter by snapping his fingers. A human who would think it a fab idea to rent a silver stretch limo for the evening. He would of course call the chauffeur *my man*.

But hold for a moment. These trousers were brown, only half as bad as black for some reason. And the fellow brought you flowers. Not many fellows bring flowers nowadays. Perhaps he simply needs a stern lecture.

Sister Soignée

■

Dear Sister Soignée:

Something tells me I'm turning into a superficial person.

I've noticed that when I wake up and put on an old sweat suit, my whole day is shot. I shamble around feeling negative and end up at home later that night eating a salisbury steak TV dinner. And I really don't like salisbury steak much.

The scenario changes drastically when I spiff myself up. My step is springy, my outlook is sunny, and I often find myself making sparkling conversation with the cute girl from accounting when we meet at the water cooler. I end my day at a chic bistro, often with that same cute girl.

I'm annoyed with myself. Outward appearance shouldn't mean so much. Why should I feel better simply because I'm wearing a dove gray cashmere sweater?

Isn't it the inner man that counts?

James

Dear James:

Let me say, with all due respect, that if you were a woman you wouldn't talk such drivel.

Only last week I was wandering about in a slough of despair. I couldn't find an outfit that made my hips look narrower than those of a smallish hippopotamus. I was inconsolable until I happened to come upon in my closet a long black skirt *already dry cleaned!* My spirits soared!

There is nothing silly about this. Frivolous, yes; but frivolity is a necessity of life.

Only men are under the mistaken impression that the personality radiates outward. We women have always known that the reverse is true. Why do you think we crave beautiful shoes? To show off our feet? No, we know that with ugly shoes on we won't be able to paint that masterpiece, or write the great American novel, or even remember to take the clothes out of the dryer.

Stop being upset with yourself. You have stumbled upon a truth of the ages.

Sister Soignée

■

Dear Sister Soignée:

I saw a picture in a magazine of a great sweater. I like this sweater a lot. It costs $500. I think this is steep. Can you think of any way for me to justify this expenditure?

Agatha

Dear Agatha:

Not unless you're a millionaire. For a normal person, this is simply too much money. If you had spent a mere (!) $200, you might someday, possibly with the help of a trained hypnotist, forget such a fatuously extravagant move. (I personally wouldn't spend more than $75 on a sweater unless it made my mouth go dry with delight.)

But spend $500 and you will be constantly reliving the experience, since such a surrealistic expenditure will undoubtedly cause a trauma. The rest of your life will then be designated as either (a) before the purchase of the $500 sweater or (b) after the purchase of the $500 sweater.

You will be driven to discuss it. Someone will say, "Nice sweater," and before you know where you are you will have said, "Not bad for $500, don't you think?" or someone else will say, "Nice weather we're having," and you'll answer, "Yes, the perfect climate for my $500 sweater."

You won't want to do this. You simply won't be able to help yourself.

Sister Soignée

■

Dear Sister Soignée:

If someone used to live with someone who wears moronic clothes, does that mean he's a moron too?

My fellow is friendly with his ex-wife, so I get to see her occasionally. You wouldn't believe the outfits.

Once at brunch she wore gold lamé knickers, a silver-threaded ruffled-within-an-inch-of-its-life blouse, and some gold doubloons hanging off one ear. Also anklets. She never actually said "Ahoy maties," but I kept expecting her to. This is only one of her fun outfits.

The woman is an eyesore. What am I doing with her ex-husband?

Flora

Dear Flora:

If you hadn't gone to brunch, you would never have had to see those gold lamé knickers. Any self-respecting human being is still in bed at this time.

But not to worry. Cleo's mother, an astute old tart, once said, "Never judge someone by who he's in love with; judge him by his friends."

People fall in love with the most appalling people. Take a cool, appraising glance at his pals.

Sister Soignée

PART THREE URBANITY

TECHNOPHILIA

I scared myself to death yesterday when I realized that the happiest moment of the day came while I was playing the bank machine.

This is a fear even scarier than the one that seized me a few years ago when I realized that with the aid of my electric blanket, my shower massage, and my Walkman, I no longer had any actual need for people. That was pretty unsettling, but my electric blanket, my shower massage, and my Walkman, although essential, meant nothing to me emotionally. They were useful objects, true, but I wasn't in love with them. I didn't want to give them kisses or marry them. They didn't make life one sweet song.

But oh, that bank machine. I just love doing it with it. The machine says, "Hello, can I help you?" and I'm in heaven with the buttons. I punch in my code and it knows me, I'm on the list. I transfer money, check my balances, make deposits, get cash. Then maybe check my balance again. I feel all calm and lofty. I commune with the machine, and the world pales to insignificance.

Just recently I discovered that I have even developed a new science. I can tell how fast a person will be at the machine by the way she's dressed!

Slowest people: women with biggish ankles wearing gauzy hippie dresses embroidered with little mirrors; men whose trouser cuffs are frayed and touch the ground; grandmothers with children in tow; anyone with uncertain hemlines or missing buttons.

Fastest people: mothers with children in tow; men in tortoiseshell glasses; anyone wearing tight jeans, a running jacket, and running shoes.

Is this psycho behavior? Sometimes I pop into a banking center for no reason, simply for the warm glow. Is this weird?

It's also weird about the buses. You know those new computerized buses where a sign flashes Please Stand Behind the White Line or Stop Requested? I'm obsessed. There's a button you can press on the back door so that it will open without you holding it. It hardly ever works. I get real excited when it does. Even more thrilling is when I press the Stop Requested button and the bus emits a little *ping* and the sign lights up. I get irritated if someone else pushes the Stop Requested button first.

My sister, a suburbanite, got a microwave oven. It has special little buttons. It will boil water, bake a potato, warm the baby's bottle, explode a poodle. It comes with a little microwave cookbook, with recipes for things like enchiladas! And there's a little "micro-go-round" sort of thing in the center that turns the food. I know I should be appalled.

"We don't ever use the stove anymore," my sister says.

"The only thing it doesn't cook is a bagel," her husband says.

My son has a calculator watch. We use it in restaurants. I read out the items from the check, he punches the amounts into his watch. Then I can say to a party of four, "I owe exactly $15.52 and I don't care if the check is $135." People hate me. I don't care.

My little under-five-pound portable typewriter that is clandestinely a computer? I adore it. I have been known to give it a discreet little kiss when no one is looking. I take it on planes with me and write, feeling terribly jet-set.

How did I ever live before I had a VCR? I get my son to tape my favorite shows for me so that I can whiz through the commercials with the remote control. It even tells time!

I'm frightened. I love to watch the letters materialize on the cable TV station that only carries computerized classified ads. The words mean nothing. I just like the typeface.

Why even mention my answering machine with its beeperless remote? Suffice it to say I would kill my own cousin before giving it up.

And the taxis. Those new ones that vomit forth receipts whether you ask for them or not.

I'm secretly convinced that computers are little people. They're friendly. My mind categorically refuses to believe that a cool, lifeless computer will cook me dinner or say "I'm sorry to have to ask, but will you tell me the last three digits of your account number?"

Something in me believes that my typewriter has a soul similar to Dorothy Parker's, and that it's proud of me every time I type something clever.

What if I'm wrong? What if all my computer play-mates are actually malevolent but just biding their time?

I can see it now. I go to the bank machine, ask it for fifty dollars. Letters appear on the screen: "Not one penny until you get that hair out of your face, call your mother, stop running around with foreigners, and find yourself a nice Jewish boy."

This could happen.

What if my pal the computerized answering machine takes offense one day and cleverly simulates my agent's voice saying "The whole deal fell through, apply for food stamps immediately."

My friend the bus could decide that I have no business visiting my friend Lucy on the Upper East Side if I'm going to persist in wearing red plastic shoes and a secondhand jacket.

The computer letters on my television set might suddenly inform me that I'm to stop listening to Joe Ely and cultivate Mantovani instead.

And I couldn't stop them. Who could?

DEVIANT SURVIVAL TIPS

I was walking along Fourteenth Street, just minding my own business, when suddenly I heard a deeply strange sound, a sort of *whop.*

The air in front of me shimmered, and then—you could have knocked me down with a feather—out of the deepest abysses of nowhere a Holy Man appeared. I could tell he was a Holy Man by his brilliantly tailored white linen robes.

"Come and know me," he said.

"Piss off, pervert," I said.

"Laudably succinct," he said, "but waste not your vitriol on me. I'm here to help you. You'll be glad you met me."

"What are you selling, buster?" I demanded.

Another man, all furtive gestures, approached us, brandishing a dagger. "Take this knife for five dollars, mama," he hissed. "A great present for your main man."

The Holy Man said, "Away with you, you infinitesimal speck of sleaze." He wiggled a hand and the man ceased to be. One minute a knife-brandishing maniac, the next, pristine empty space.

"Where'd he go?" I asked.

"I move in mysterious ways, my wonders to perform, for I am Mahatma Grossman, the Holy Man," the Holy Man said. "And I have chosen you to spread the word. These downtown urban beings—always they run! Never do they go anywhere!—must learn survival. You will be my vessel. I will fill you with knowledge."

"Mahatma Grossman?" I mused.

"It is I," he said. "I am wondrous."

"Why me?"

"Who can say? You are wearing a very nice belt. Now will you please whip out the little notebook I am sure you carry, write down every word I say, and communicate my thoughts to the masses."

What follows is an exact transcription of his words.

O downtown urban beings, hear my words and follow my instructions to the letter.

Number one: Never listen to anybody. What do they know? Every being wants to be very cool, he wants at all times to chill out. But too many beings will try to set rules for chilling out.

You are the one with the chilled-out hair, they will tell you, or, You are so chilled out and cynical.

And it does not pay to listen! Or you will forever be cultivating your chilled-out hair, teasing it into shapes that turn the stomach. And you are so taken with your chilled-out cynicism that it overtakes all else. So your face is nothing but a palsy of lip-curling.

I say, to be chilled out, keep your own counsel.

["How much does it cost to get those robes dry-cleaned?" I asked him. "You will please shut up," he said.]

Number two: Stay away from all new kids in town.

For new kids are invariably hustlers. They come to the big city to make it big. And before the big city has beaten them into submission, they are forever obnoxious.

The new kids have convinced themselves that

the city is all about who you know, *about* connections. *Always they want people to take them
to parties.*

*Parties at which—if they want to be "in film,"
they'll meet Jack Nicholson, they think. And Jack
Nicholson will be entranced immediately and give
them his phone number and say come for lunch
next Tuesday and by the way would you like to
co-star in my next movie?*

*This connections business is only a new-kid
fantasy. But a new kid won't believe you if you
tell him that. He will try to oil his way everywhere and introduce himself madly to any being
whom he thinks can help his pathetic career.
"You're invited to Cosima von Bülow's party?"
he will breathe in awe. "Oh, take me, please
take me."*

*"Well, not that Cosima von Bülow," you will
say. "This is another Cosima von Bülow, whose
father owns a dry cleaners in Queens."*

*"Oh dear," will say the new kid. "I think I have
to wash my hair that night."*

*We oldsters know that there is only one way to
"make it" in the city, and that is to work yourself
to death. And then work some more. Sticking to
one thing all the while.*

*No new kid can come here and decide he will
be in films or maybe a performance artist or possibly a video producer or how about a museum
curator.*

He will starve.

*Number three: Let people push you around. The
being who says, believes, and acts on the phrase I*
ain't taking any shit from nobody *is a very busy
being indeed.*

*For he must be ever-vigilant against the news
vendor who shortchanges him, the cab driver who
takes him the long way around, the waiter who*

serves another being first, the florist who is charging ten cents more for a tulip than the other florist down the street, the pharmacist who makes him wait too long, the drivers of automobiles who cut him off at the light. A being who concerns himself with such trivia becomes a veritable miasma of righteous indignation and never has a minute to relax and have a good time.

The city is a combat zone, and everyone must have an angle or he is not allowed over the bridges or through the tunnels to this great mecca. You must let them have their angles; it is what they live for. You are better off pursuing your own angles, such as ensuring that your loved ones don't try any funny stuff. You may lose a few pennies on excess taxi fare or tulip overcharge, but you will save a fortune in brain wear-and-tear.

["Did your mother name you Mahatma?" I wondered. He gave me a look that shriveled my innards.]

Number four: Steer clear of overviews. Many beings may have the situation of Lebanon in perspective. Others know exactly how to plot a campaign for gay rights. Others are well versed in the strategies of corporate takeovers. And yet they are morons.

For God's will to be performed, it must be in ever-widening circles. Someone who understands the situation in Lebanon but who forgets to call his best friend who just had a root canal is lost to the right priorities. He will also snap at his offspring when they have innocent homework problems; he will not notice when his lover has a deadline. Enlightenment begins at home. Start there.

Homework, root canals, and deadlines are the sacred details of life. One must understand and be properly in awe of these details, for God is *always to be found at the back of the refrigerator behind the moldy tuna fish casserole, or sometimes He is found in the way the tailor at your corner lovingly stitches up the hem of your party dress, other times in the way a child sings along with a toothpaste commercial. Do not look for him in the heavens; he only keeps a small locker there, only goes there to change.*

Only when one's own house is in order may one then presume to look at the larger questions.

Number five: When in doubt, make a fool of yourself. This Mick Jagger, he prances around, makes funny faces, wears silly clothes! He is a millionaire! He trusts his cosmic intuition! He has no market researchers who do plenty of audience surveys and then tell him "jump more to the left at a 45-degree angle. Wear a puce body stocking." This Mick Jagger plunges into the depth of his being and he then comes up dancing like a chicken: He is not afraid.

A comedian is not funny unless he is taking his demons out for a walk. An actor is a wooden doll unless he lets us see what most would rather hide. And nobody can make a Steven Spielberg movie except Steven Spielberg. Amen.

"So wait—that's it?" I asked.

"I am tired. I have thirst," he said.

"You're ending on the Steven Spielberg note?"

"I will be gracious and give you one more piece of wonderment," he said. "Don't take any wooden nickels." And with another *whop,* he was gone.

EXHAUSTION THERAPY

Oh, we try, do we ever try. We slog through the streets—running to the deli, scampering to the post office, trotting up to our office, dashing to pick up the laundry.

We are urban superpeople on the move. We have to be; it's our job. Anyone who doesn't race through the days and nights like a gazelle on speed doesn't belong in the city. Even the country and small small towns have little, although more, use for layabouts. So if you regularly find that you have time for a volleyball game and are accustomed to baking random batches of cookies simply to fill your time, you're not keeping your end up.

But there *are* limits. Every once in a while, even superpeople must turn to themselves and say, "I'm tired."

When the dread tiredness strikes, it takes no prisoners. You'd better listen to it; only at peril to your very soul can you wake up at 8 A.M., spend three hours composing a sonata, do a couple of hours of aerobics, attend a hard-hitting business lunch, spend the afternoon directing a feature film, fly to Boston for dinner, and fly back to attend a dance party until 3 A.M. If you do this when you don't feel like it, you'll get a headache.

Then your back will go out. Then you'll start seeing funny spots before your eyes. Then you'll develop a rash in a highly confidential area. Then you'll start having funny dreams. Then you'll somehow convince yourself that your lover is turning bisexual.

This should be the starting point of exhaustion therapy. The minute you first suspect that your lover has become bisexual, close up shop. Turn the phone off, turn up the music, get into bed, and call it a day.

Don't even leave your answering machine on. If you do, you will inevitably be tempted to get out of bed to monitor the messages. And as sure as you're born, your agent will call and say that Goldie Hawn cannot live another day unless you immediately begin writing a movie for her.

You don't need this. What you need is a cup of tea and a stack of magazines. Maybe a couple of cozy murder mysteries. Possibly a warm and friendly body.

No, possibly not. Warm and friendly bodies tend to want attention. If they're being all cute and cuddly, and you're staring off into space like the Duke of Edinburgh on downs, the w & f body may fall into a snit, and the last thing one needs when one is exhausted is a tense and sulking body. Even a small tiff could sap the vital juices to the point of no return.

Exhaustion therapy should last approximately one week, two for severe cases. During the first three days a strict regimen must be followed, consisting of bed rest, television watching, light reading, and teenage eating.

It is crucial to eat teenage while tired. Things like roast beef on rye, a bag of potato chips, and a Coke from the deli (have them deliver) will comfort you. Also nice are pizza, orange juice mixed with club soda, olives, and spaghetti. No drinking, no drugs. You can do it.

Make sure you realize that you are simply tuckered out, not depressed. If you think you're depressed you'll start eating Oreos, chocolate-chocolate chip ice cream, and marshmallow fluff. Then, when you attempt to get out of bed again, the weight of your thighs will keep you pinned to the sheets.

After three days you can make phone calls to friends and eat at the coffee shop on the corner. But no errands, no business.

After five days you can gently test the waters. Dinner out, maybe. And the next day perhaps a business lunch as long as you have a long nap afterward. The next day you may be cured.

It's depressing, but the world will live all too happily without you for a few days. It won't even notice you're gone, which is why anyone with a career may never stay exhausted for more than two weeks without running the risk of finding that one has vanished without a trace. (YOU: Hello, Agent! How are you? I've been pretty tired for a while, but now I'm right as rain and ready to start working on that Goldie movie. AGENT: Nice to hear from you. Let's have lunch. Good-bye.)

There are some wonderful side effects to deciding that you're having an exhaustion attack:

- You don't have to go to cocktail parties.
- Since no one is going to see you, you don't have to get your legs waxed or shave.
- Or wash your hair.
- You won't be riding on the bus next to a man who is constantly muttering, "Those fucking assholes they told me they would kill me I'm gonna get them with a shotgun and blow their heads off the fucking goddamned cocksuckers they're gonna die and then Lorna will be sorry, then she'll know..."
- You won't run into anyone at a restaurant who says, "My goodness, don't you look healthy! Have you gained a little weight?"
- No traffic jams.
- You won't be in clothing shops where the salesgirl will force you to try on a fun fur.

But mainly, you won't have to think. And not thinking can be the most wonderful experience on earth, leading, in fact, to nirvana.

CO-OP OWNERSHIP: FACT OR NIGHTMARE?

The story started simply enough: If I didn't buy my apartment, I would be evicted. "You fools!" I remember yelling to the other tenants in the building. "We're only paying three hundred dollars a month! If we co-op, we'll be paying double! Triple! For what? For these same ratholes!" Nobody listened. They talked equity. Thus was I dragged kicking and screaming into home-ownership and the associate yuppiehood.

Needless to say, I have since become insufferable, preening among friends and often informing chance passersby on the street what a clever girl I am, I own a co-op. But one should not be fooled by my sunny demeanor. It is simply a perverse reaction to lifelong imprisonment.

Consider: owning a co-op is only desirable if you want to leave town. Buy it at an insider's price, sell it for a million dollars, leave the city and buy the Taj Majal. Otherwise buy at an insider's price, decide to move, sell your apartment for a million dollars, and find out that your profit barely covers a down payment on another place at an outsider's price. Or you could decide to rent with your profits. Ha ha. Ever tried to rent an apartment in a city in which there *are* no rental apartments, like Manhattan? The going rate on a cock-roach-infested broom closet is two thousand dollars a month, excluding utilities.

The same thing could happen to you at any moment, so read on. There are other pitfalls to co-op ownership besides complete financial enslavement. Here are just a few things to steel yourself against:

1 PERCENTAGES Your maintenance will be maybe 68% tax deductible. Your mortgage is, oh, 11¼% this year, with a 5% cap which is dependent on T-bills plus 2½%, and the most it can fluctuate is 3% a year. Your real estate lawyer charges 1% under $100,000, ½% over. The broker charges 6%, the flip tax is 10%. The bank origination fee is 3½%...

The probability of ever thinking creatively again is 14%. Your day will be comprised of 20% anxiety, 32% severe hopelessness, 40% fear, and 8% blind hope.

2 THE CO-OP MEETING These are always called on the night you've booked a nonrefundable flight to Rio, but you'd better stay home, since if you don't everyone there will vote to make your apartment into a beauty salon. Meetings are held in the apartment of your worst enemy, who doesn't serve coffee. Everyone smokes, but you will be the only one with cigarettes. If you leave the room for a second, your downstairs neighbor will entertain the others with a tape recording of your most recent romantic interlude. Somebody will want to know where the fuse box is, which will prompt a lively discussion on the possibility of rewiring the entire building. Two hours later this will be proved unfeasible. Then fuel bills will be discussed at length, culminating in a fistfight between the guy who wants to join a fuel co-op and another guy who calls the first guy a commie.

Then, for comic relief, you will be nominated to join the co-op board.

3 THE CO-OP BOARD On no account join this. In the first heady flush of excitement, you may feel all est-like and want to be responsible for your own destiny, but resist this impulse heroically.

Otherwise every night before you go to bed a neighbor will call to tell you the front door is broken again and two vagrants have set up light housekeeping in the hallway. You will be awakened every morning by another neighbor who thinks she smells gas, and each workday will be punctuated with calls from other hysterical board members calling to announce that the woman who smelled gas called Con Ed instead of the plumber and now the gas is turned off and there's no heat or hot water and there won't be any until the inspector from Con Ed comes back, but he won't come back until a city inspector has preceded him, and nobody knows what number to call to get the city inspector but even if they could get it Con Ed says it will probably take a month for the second inspector to come and everybody's got to be home every day until they do come because each apartment has to be examined before the gas can be turned back on and they can't really say when they'll come, sometime between 6:30 A.M. and 9 P.M., so maybe the thing to do would be for everyone to leave their keys with the vagrants who are living in the hallway.

4 BECOMING HOUSE-PROUD Suddenly the fact that you have the ugliest bathroom sink in existence will become intolerable. You, who heretofore only concerned yourself with the cut of your jacket, will be perusing plumbing catalogs and driving out to auctions in New Jersey just in case you may find a turn-of-the-century Victorian-influenced claw-footed brass-fauceted bathroom sink. When the ultimate sink is found, you'll realize you need entirely new bathroom accessories, otherwise known as towel racks. Being thus obsessed, you will forget about your own appearance for weeks at a time, and be startled one day when you catch sight of yourself in a random mirror in an appliance store and discover that you have put on ten pounds, the black roots of your red hair are now an inch long, and you have a large grease stain on your sweater.

Meanwhile the guy who lives above you will decide he can't live another day unless his apartment is completely gutted and redone in a high-tech manner. He will employ two hippie workmen who spend every morning ripping out the floorboards above your head while playing the same Grateful Dead tape over and over and who become completely unhinged when the half-ton black bathtub the guy upstairs wanted takes them an hour to hump up two flights of stairs and when they finally make it up there they drop the bathtub in disgust which is too much for a floor lacking boards so while you're minding your own business brushing your teeth the ceiling above you crumbles about your shoulders and the bottom of a half-ton black bathtub heaves into view, where it stays for six weeks, because both hippie workmen decide to go back to Ann Arbor and the two Rasta workmen that your neighbor hires instead think the bathtub looks nice that way. Sort of artistic.

5 INSURANCE You must have some! The guy above you forgot to buy any. You didn't forget but every time you tried to read the policy you felt faint, so when the bathtub crashes in who's going to pay for the ceiling? Not you, that's for sure, but your neighbor says it really isn't his fault either, not really if you think about it. It's those two hippies from Ann Arbor and why should he be responsible for them, so you have to call a meeting of the board but no one will come because they've all gone to Rio.

6 NAMELESS FEARS What if the building burns down? What if it goes bankrupt? What, precisely, does *bankrupt* mean? Is there insurance against bankruptcy? Do you have to read the policy?

7 RAMPANT ACQUISITIVENESS One day you will look around you and realize that you and your two loved ones are living in 400 square feet, and even though you've lived there for ten years, suddenly you won't be able to breathe. You will start prowling through real estate sections of the newspaper and find yourself dazzled by such poetry as "2 bed, 2 bth, stdy, grdn vu,

EIK, WBFP, LOW MAINT! A steal at 350K!" You toy briefly with the idea of selling your firstborn into white slavery, but become despondent when you discover that the going rate for young boys is only 150K, only enough for a small one-bedroom in Hell's Kitchen. But then the sister-in-law of your hairdresser's boyfriend sends a message that there is a two-bedroom apartment going real cheap, with only minor problems—an electrical fire last month, most of the tenants on rent strike, the building hasn't exactly gone co-op yet but it probably definitely will, most of the view is an airshaft, it's a fifth-floor walkup, and the owner is a paranoid schizophrenic—but otherwise perfect!

This information fills you with such *joie de vivre* that you put your apartment up for sale immediately. And for the first time you know *real* trouble.

APARTMENT DRAMA

Scene i: *A woman is circling, caged-tigerlike, around a small but colorful four-room apartment. She is wearing a forlorn cotton nightgown and is brandishing a meat cleaver. A naked man is hiding behind a large green chair. A bowl of cereal and some grapes are on a fold-down table. Unfolded laundry festoons a sofa.*

SHE· Pack your things, you sex fiend! I want you out of here, you Lothario! Pervert! Serpent!

HE· Jesus, hon, put that cleaver down. You could hurt somebody.

SHE· I can't wait to see your brains spill out all over the carpet!

HE· Now, now. I told you I never saw that card before

in my life. The stewardess must have slipped it into my pocket while I wasn't looking.

SHE· Pull the other one, you rat-faced swine.

HE· You're overreacting.

SHE· Overreacting??!! I'll show you overreacting, you pea-brained twit!

(She lunges with the cleaver, missing him by inches. He jumps over the chair and grabs the cleaver-wielding wrist. They scuffle until the doorbell rings.)

SHE· Shit. *(Goes to intercom)* Who is it?

INTERCOM VOICE· Bennet from Planet Realty.

(They stare at each other for one dismayed second. Then she turns to the table, grabs the bowl of cereal and rushes into the kitchen, from where we hear a sudden surge of water and the clatter of crockery. Meanwhile he begins frantically folding laundry, throwing confusing things like lace panties behind the sofa. A gentle tap sounds at the front door. The man looks down, notices his genitals, and runs into the bedroom. The woman answers the door. A pleasant-faced man and a woman wearing a bow tie enter.)

SHE· Hi there! Excuse the nightgown. I, uh, ha ha ha.

PLEASANT FACE· Why don't I show you the bedroom first?

BOW TIE· That would be nice.

SHE· No! I mean ha ha. How about the kitchen? Great kitchen. Note the hanging plant. Thrown in, gratis. You'll probably want to get one of those half-refrigerators and double your counter space, ho ho. These urban kitchens.

BOW TIE· How much of the maintenance is tax deductible?

SHE· Oh, surely 66 percent.

BOW TIE· You get much light?

SHE· Oodles, actually. I've been known to iron with sunglasses on.

BOW TIE· Cable TV?

SHE· For days.

BOW TIE· What percentage of shares do you own?

SHE· Well, with one thing and another—(*The man emerges from the bedroom wearing running shorts and a frilly pink bed jacket.*) Oh hello, darling! Isn't he cute?

HE· Come in, come in. I was just uh. Well. Hello!

(*Bow tie soundlessly inspects bedroom, bathroom, kitchen, and a room containing 32 stuffed animals, 7892 baseball cards, 4 saxophones, 7 guitars, 2 clarinets, 1 flute, and a dulcimer.*)

BOW TIE· Closets?

SHE· Plenty! Three, in fact. But you won't want to open them, they're ah...

HE· A bit under the weather. Indisposed. Rather full up.

SHE· (*Sudden burst.*) It's a wonderful apartment! I wrote a book here!

HE· So did I!

PLEASANT FACE· There's a washer-dryer in the basement.

BOW TIE· Yes. Thank you. I'll let you know. Goodbye. (*They exit.*)

SHE· Wrote a book here, did you, my angel? And what are you wearing? Get my bed jacket off immediately. This is not transvestite central.

HE· You've hidden all my clothes. Why have you hidden all my clothes?

Sʜᴇ· There isn't room. We have to give the appearance of spaciousness. (*Her brow suddenly clouds.*) Anyway, I don't want you here. Go. Pack.

Hᴇ· How can I pack if I can't find my clothes?

(*She picks up the cleaver again, starts after him. The doorbell rings.*)

Sᴄene ii: *Later that night, 3* A.M. *Man and woman are in bed, asleep. Suddenly she sits up with a start and screams.*

Hᴇ· (*Mumbling abstractedly.*) I swear it, I never saw it before. Anyway that stewardess had legs like a piano. Good night, dear.

Sʜᴇ· What if we don't sell? We've put a deposit down on another apartment! We'll be in the street! You'll be living in the men's shelter and I'll be a bag lady!

Hᴇ· We'll sell.

Sʜᴇ· No, we won't. People want doormen! People want elevators!

Hᴇ· Fuck doormen! Fuck elevators. This is the Village, baby. This is where we all come to find our way. Walk down our street, you hear actors rehearsing, painters painting, pianists practicing. It's a charmed life.

Sʜᴇ· Good night, you beast.

Hᴇ· Good night, you cow.

LOVE AFFAIRS

THE WALKING WOUNDED

We, the walking wounded, are a band of merry marauders, laying waste to tender psyches in cities, boroughs, and hamlets all over the land.

Once victims of severe damage while engaging in the war between the sexes, we take no prisoners. We strike, destroy, and flee. We recognize no DMZs.

And we are clever. When we find a potential victim, we pretend to be all warm and wonderful and loving and caring and vulnerable. And then, as our victim succumbs to our wiles, we laugh mirthlessly and say, "So sorry, but you're more ready for a commitment than I am," or, when really going for the jugular, "Sorry, but I've fallen in love with someone else." Then we whistle a careless tune and evaporate into the night, one more scalp hanging from our belts.

You probably know us. You may well be one of us. If so, you know we weren't always this way. Witness the case histories of some of our jolly band:

FRED

Fred was no fun at all until he met Myra. Withdrawn and meek, he would stare into space at parties, then go home and make a Spam sandwich for a midnight snack. His only sexual encounters were with random hookers, whom he would implore to beat him. But they wouldn't, since discipline was extra.

Then Myra breezed into Fred's life. No feast for the

eyes, dear Myra—too tall, lank hair, fattish thighs. But she had a sweet vulnerability in her deep green eyes that Fred went for in a big way.

Before he knew where he was, Fred had turned into a cliché: walking hand in hand in the park, making love in front of a roaring fire, giggling. Fred was happy for the first time in his life.

One day Myra failed to show up for a date. When Fred called, Myra explained sweetly that she was terribly sorry, but she had met a really dreamy mountain climber and she was moving to Switzerland with him.

EVE

Eve was really excited about Tony. She never had to tell him anything twice. He always got the point, the joke, the cruel irony. Plus she could jump on him anytime, anyplace, and he was ready. Even on the beach, her favorite place.

But one morning Tony wasn't ready. He got up quickly, put his clothes on, and left with a hasty "Got to meet my mother for lunch."

When she ran into him later that day, hand in hand with a dazzling blonde, he was at a loss for words for the first time in his life.

She forgave him once, twice, three times. He did it again, again, again.

HOWIE

Howie's mother hated him. It had been a difficult birth, and in his formative years Howie's mother was fond of lifting up her blouse, showing Howie her scars, and whining, "Look what you've done to me."

Howie's first marriage fizzled, but when he met Pam, he decided to try again. Pam needed him. He was going to help her get off drugs and enroll her in acting class. He and Pam went to Vegas to get married. They took a few grams of cocaine and a couple of thousand dollars. Soon the cocaine was gone and the money spent.

"Why don't we go to bed now?" Howie prompted.

"Why don't you go and fuck yourself," Pam shouted, throwing her wedding ring at him.

STEPHANIE

Stephanie met Fred in the Laundromat. He was having trouble sorting his whites; she counseled him. Fred was shy and withdrawn, which Stephanie found appealing. They started dating. Stephanie didn't mind sharing Fred's passion for Spam sandwiches, although she did try to introduce him to nitrate-free bacon.

One day Stephanie waited for Fred for an hour in front of the movie theater where they had planned to see *Rocky VII.*

"What happened to you?" she asked Fred when she finally reached him on the telephone.

"I was there at the appointed time," he said stonily. "I didn't wait."

"Why not? I was only five minutes late, I had trouble getting a cab."

"Don't give me that shit," said Fred. "You women are all alike. Think you can walk all over a man."

"Huh?" said Stephanie.

JEFF

"Thank God I've finally met the woman of my dreams," thought Jeff as he gazed into Eve's eyes.

"What are you staring at?" Eve snapped.

"I was just thinking how beautiful you are and how much I love you," said Jeff.

"Sure," said Eve, "and whose face were you gazing into *last* night?"

"Huh?" said Jeff. "I told you I had a late meeting."

"You must think I was born yesterday," said Eve. "Get lost, creep."

CANDY

Candy realized she was falling for Howie, and the thought gave her a misty glow.

Howie bought her son presents and told Candy how her delicate wrists made him want to protect her. He called her three, four times a day just to say hello. He was sweet.

But one night at dinner Howie was strangely silent, although Candy noticed a mad glint in his eyes. Just as they were tucking into their bread pudding, Howie said he had a bad stomachache and had to go straight home. "I'll come with you," said Candy. "No," said Howie.

"Howie, is something wrong?" asked Candy when she saw him again.

"Not really."

"Of course, how silly of me. 'Not really.' Do you mean anything special by that?"

"Well," said Howie, "now that you mention it, I happen to think you're growing too attached to me. I think maybe we should stop seeing each other."

"Huh?" said Candy.

"It's for the best," said Howie.

"Rubbish. Tell me another one. I'm crazy about you. I'm sticking to you like glue."

"You don't understand, Candy. I'm a member of the walking wounded. I've been hurt too much—now I only delight in hurting other people. I'm a classic case."

"Oh, I see. So now I'm supposed to assume a hurt and shocked expression, maybe burst into tears. Pretend to be a deer frozen in the headlights?"

"Candy, I'm being serious, goddamnit!"

"So am I, my prince. You're not getting rid of me so easily. If you want me out of your life, you'll have to procure some little-known Asiatic poison."

Candy's behavior was disastrous to the morale of the walking wounded. Nobody had ever broken formation like she did, nobody had ever laughed in our faces and refused to take our pain seriously. For a while there was dissension in the ranks. A small, well-organized band of rebels wanted to break away and again try to form decent, lasting love affairs. But somehow it all came to nothing.

HOW TO FIGHT WITH A LOVED ONE

Love is funny. Ha ha. One week you and your loved one have discovered the shape of the universe within your relationship—conversation is harmonious, glances are tender, discreet gropings in taxicabs are blissful.

Then, the next week, somebody does something or, just as likely, nobody does anything, but nevertheless chaos reigns. Silences become stony and sullen, eyes hooded and secretive, chance remarks disastrously misunderstood. Tiny differences are suddenly canyons of distrust and resentment. Then comes the grisly internal dialogue: "Good God, how can I *be* with this person! She has no idea who I am! She doesn't get my jokes! She has absolutely no interest in quantum physics! She never remembers the Dead Parrot sketch! I'm trapped! Life is over!"

Life is not over; life is just irritating. To stay alive, all love affairs must keep moving and will therefore often careen into rocky, bleak chasms when you're not looking. It is a scientific law that whenever you're feeling resentful and mean, your partner is feeling equally ratty, and you will fight. To keep bloodshed and love affair fatalities to a minimum, please follow these rules:

1 NEVER FIGHT WHEN YOU COULD BE SLEEPING   If you're capable of dozing off, do it. The only grievances worth airing are the ones that actually keep you awake. All others will seem a lot more trivial come the bright morn.

2 WHENEVER POSSIBLE, GIVE IN   Fighting is grueling and time consuming. Heated words often have awful syntax. When being attacked, think beautiful thoughts. Remember how sweet your lover was the day you had the appendectomy. Only counterattack when every shred of dignity you have to spare has been stripped away. Then try something like, "Why yes, darling, you're probably right about my having no brain to speak of and impersonating a sick halibut while talking to your boss at the Christmas party, but remember how pleasant I am to your gerbils."

3 THE THIRD TIME YOU PUT ON YOUR SHOES AND COAT, YOU MUST ACTUALLY LEAVE   Nobody respects a Ping-Pong ball. One cannot be constantly leaping off one's sofa shouting, "That's absolutely it! I can't stand this anymore!" and then storming out the door if one keeps reappearing three seconds later, saying, "And another thing..."

4 SENTENCES YOU MUST NEVER UTTER DURING A FIGHT   "You've never really loved me."
"I've never really loved you."
"Your penis is minuscule."
"Your thighs make me puke."
"If you cared anything for me, you'd give up this selfish notion of becoming a neurosurgeon."
"It's all your mother's fault."
"I wish I were dead."
"Are you asleep?"

5 DO NOT SNIVEL   Even your own child will curl his lip contemptuously if you whimper and say things like, "After all I've done for you, you could think of *me* for a change."

6 IF YOU FIND YOURSELF FIGHTING IN BED, YOU'RE NOT GETTING ENOUGH SEX   The line between lust and anger is thin. Sometimes you think you're in the throes of one when in reality you simply need a bit of the other. Remedy this immediately.

7 EVEN DURING PEACETIME, INDULGE IN SAUCY BADINAGE   The light of my existence just sauntered by, looking exhilarating in boxer shorts, and started reading over my shoulder. "Why don't you tell them what a prince I am to put up with a mentally deranged and compulsively frivolous writer," he said.

"I'll tell them what it's like to become involved with a pigheaded male supremacist from Down Under, you loathsome excrescence," I said.

"Want a cup of tea, you horrible old tart?" he wondered.

"Yes, please, pencil dick."

It is possible these terms of endearment are not for everybody. But we have learned that insults not only diffuse the tensions inherent in intimacy, they are also more fun than saying "Oh baby oh baby."

8 SHOULD YOU NOTICE YOURSELF TURNING INTO YOUR MOTHER, SHUT UP IMMEDIATELY   This can happen to any of us at any time. There we will be, minding our own business, when suddenly macabre words spring to our lips, words that make absolutely no sense but seem bound and determined to be said. They seem vaguely familiar, these words, as well they should, since our subconscious has been taking a trip down memory lane and we are repeating the exact words our mother or father said twenty years ago. Most inappropriate.

When this occurs, take a cold shower, tape your mouth closed, anything. Otherwise your life will turn into a repeating tape loop.

9 ALWAYS ANSWER THE PHONE DURING A FIGHT   Nothing thwarts heated insanity more than the voice of a cool, calm third party wondering if you're free for lunch next Tuesday.

10 BEFORE YOU KISS AND MAKE UP, MAKE SURE THE FIGHT IS REALLY OVER   People who love each other will often pretend that everything is okay when they are still secretly seething. This leads to prolonged resentment, what I like to call the Superbowl Syndrome.

"The kid doesn't like it when you write about him," says my larger loved one, again reading over my shoulder.

"Just don't tell him," I snap.

Superbowl '83, it was. I made a monumental mistake. I bet the kid that the Raiders would win. Every morning for a week before the game, the kid would wake me up saying, "Mom, you might as well give me that five dollars now, since you know the Redskins *rock the house.*"

Way before halftime, our Superbowl party was sadly flat. We had the corn chips and beer and the bag of confetti as usual, but the Raiders were winning. I was pretending to cheer halfheartedly. The kid sat there glumly; the corn chips just lay there.

It thus occurred to me that it doesn't matter if you win or lose, as long as you're rooting for the same team. The kid and I had always been on the same side before; we'd always had a terrific Superbowl.

In love affairs, when resentments fester, the same sort of thing happens.

"Aren't you stretching a bit for a parallel?" now wonders the smartass from Down Under.

"Absolutely not. You remember our last big fight. I was so goddamned furious with you that the original issue was totally beside the point. I just wanted to win. Bad. You felt the same way. You wanted to kick my face in. We were no longer on the same team. We were like a defensive tackle and a guard telling each other obscene things about each other's sister."

"It was all your fault."

"Shut up. Who cares? All I know is, once you're on opposing teams, each needing desperately to win, it's the end of a love affair. This is what resentment does. It poisons everything. To get over it you have to fight bitterly, hoist every grievance, however vague, into the air and salute it. Then when it's over you can like each other again."

"Shut up."

"Piss off."

"Come here."

11 IF YOU NOTICE THAT A FIGHT IS ALL YOUR FAULT, ADMIT IT What the hell, life is short.

WHAT IS THIS THING CALLED SPACE?

I'm sitting here, praying he doesn't come home. Wherever he is, whatever he's doing, please, God, let him do it for just a few minutes longer. A couple of hours, say. All right, an hour will do in a pinch, even half. Just a couple more minutes and I'll be fine.

What do you figure I'm doing? Boning up for my neurosurgery exam? Putting the finishing touches on a gelignite bomb? Constructing a complicated soufflé?

I'm just sitting around picking my nose. When that gets tedious, I start fastidiously scraping the paint off my toenails. For a treat I light a few cigarettes and consider making toast.

But I don't want him here, even though I love him insanely. So what if he's tall and gorgeous and will give any and every bum on the street his last quarter? So what if he's got the greenest eyes, the blackest lashes, and can play "Little Red Corvette" on the saxophone? So what if he is amusing?

Yesterday I walked in to discover that he was counting a hefty stack of money. "Darling! Where did it come from?" I wondered. "Well, sweetheart, it finally happened," he said. "I won a big dick contest."

Also he has been known to bring me flowers. Under duress, but still. But ask me if I care. No, I do not; not at the moment. What I care about is that this toad of a man refuses to put caps on anything. I am worked up into a furious lather over the uncapped shampoo, vitamins, ketchup, honey, shaving cream. And he refuses to wrap up the bread after he uses it. And when he leaves the kitchen after making breakfast, every single cupboard is open! He leaves wet towels on the sofa. And mountains of glutinous herb tea in our only teapot.

Don't tell me I'm an idiot. I know. A petty, insipid, seventies cliché of an idiot. I may as well devote my life to fashioning macramé plant holders.

I know what I'm talking about here is space. As in "I need my" or "Gimme some." I may be an idiot, but I'm no fool, and I know the main reason I'm sitting here scraping at my toenails is that this dream man, this angel in human shape, is giving me claustrophobia. Toothpaste caps, forsooth! What right-minded girl ever concerns herself with such trivia?

Me, that's who, and I'm really humiliated. Space is a concept redolent of encounter groups, self-improvement courses, hot-tub therapy, and all those other cult-of-the-self things that manage to be simultaneously mindless and pretentious. I personally think soul searching is the sort of thing you do when there's nothing on the late show and there are no mystery novels in the house, or when you're fourteen and don't know why you're horny. Loving others, that's the ticket. Feeling connected, warm-blooded, responsible yet irreverent, humble yet freewheeling—these are the things I hold dear.

But please don't let him come in right now. I'm feeling anxious. I'm getting a headache.

I'm not the only one. Rita is crazy about Herb because she only sees him on weekends. Another friend just broke up with her husband of six years and wakes up every morning feeling immense relief. She's in love with a musician in Los Angeles now—he's three thousand miles away—and she couldn't be more jolly.

I phoned Neville tonight, asked him how Lucy was. "She's out right now," he said. "We're getting along brilliantly, but I'm sitting here dreading her coming in."

"Me too! What's the matter with us? Lots of people live together forever, but can you imagine being with someone for twenty years? Or forty? How is it done?"

"There's something wrong with our generation," Neville said mournfully. "Perhaps we were all, as babies, dropped regularly on our heads. Perhaps it was a craze. 'Mothers: It's ten o'clock. Have you dropped your baby on its head today?'"

Is Neville on to something? Each generation has its own collective neuroses, which its children have no choice but to react against. Baby boom children had parents who were all madly methodical, hygienic, security-minded, ritualistic, and, let's go out on a wild psychological limb here, anal compulsive. We were fed every four hours, toilet trained by sixteen months, kept out of public swimming pools. And we're all nuts.

We hate discipline, we hate authority, we hate to do dishes, we hate being supervised. We all fall madly in love, then madly out of love. We rush in where angels fear to tread, then hotfoot it right out of there when the going gets weird, blabbering about space.

Space! Communists don't concern themselves with space—they're all living six to a bedroom. Those involved in the London blitz never mentioned space; they just passed the hot soup and bandages. Children love sleep-over parties, where eight or nine of them cram into one sleeping bag and giggle. But I, for one, become a sniveling wimp if one stunning man encroaches on my turf.

My theory: all of us inner-space seekers have been stunted in our development. All that discipline and germ fear have arrested us in the stage of fourteen-year-old horniness and rebellion.

Consider the fourteen-year-old: pimply, gangly, gum-chewing, constantly jerking off. Not child, not adult, a miasma of insecurity and hormones. The most distinguishing characteristic of the fourteen-year-old is that she or he has *no* distinguishing characteristics. All hate their parents, all listen to the same rock and roll, none would be caught dead in other than the identical clothes their peers wear. They buy anything TV tells them to. They make frenzied dashes toward independence, then get scared and rush shivering back under Mommy's wing. They're stubborn, wrong-headed, moody.

I'm still like this. My personality lacks shape. I'm continually wondering if I like the Rolling Stones or what my favorite color is. It isn't space I'm desperate for, it's definition.

People like me have fraught relationships. If we haven't a clue to what we're really like, the logical thing is to look to the person next to us in bed to tell us.

My lover is gripped by the mysteries of Stonehenge. I am not a Stonehenge sort of person, yet often I feel the need to be equally gripped. He likes Celtic music and suddenly, so do I. My personality, still searching for a shape, assumes his. I depend on him to tell me who I am.

Then I become crazed and panicky and claustrophobic. My own dependence sickens me. I cling closer and enjoy it less. His presence becomes overpowering, all-encompassing, and please let me out of here.

Give me some space or I'll break your face.

WHAT MAKES WOMEN TICK?

'T was a hot and fetid night in downtown Manhattan. Rita and I sat drinking in the humid darkness of the Lion's Head, a bar known for its hard-bitten reporters, colorful literary failures, aspiring actors, and sozzled Irishmen. Cleo was late, so we waited and watched a woman in an appalling turquoise dress sashay through the bar.

"Don't you wish," I said to Rita, "that you could just pull certain people to one side and say, 'Can we discuss your outfit for a moment, please? I think you should reconsider.'"

"Absolutely," Rita said. "The woman is an eyesore. I see her in putty-colored cotton jersey, just a little blusher, and her hair back to its natural color."

"Yo," said Cleo, finally appearing, "what's up? Dissecting that turquoise number with the clown makeup? I see her in pale peach linen."

"Listen," I said, "I need your help. As you know, I am a writer."

"As we know, you lie around on your couch all day reading fashion magazines and pretending to be looking for material," said Rita.

"We like to leave you with your little illusions," said Cleo.

"I want to write about women and how they relate to men."

"And you want our help?" asked Rita. "Why should we discuss our thoughts about men so you can steal our words and concepts, as usual?"

"I don't want men to know what I think," Cleo said.

"Don't be silly," I said. "Men and women are no longer enemies. We've reached a new plateau in the women's movement. We need to *understand* each other, be *generous* with each other—"

"Excuse me, ladies," said a dapper man in a Burberry who materialized at our table. "May my friends and I join you?"

"Get lost, creep," I said. "Anyway, if men knew what makes us tick, if they understood our little foibles—"

"Foibles?" said Rita. "Pardon me, but *foibles*? What foibles are these?"

"Okay, so maybe not foibles," I said hastily. "But you know the things they complain about—we're always late; we can never make up our minds; we never care about baseball standings; we get jealous all the time; we hate for them to go out drinking; all we care about are dresses and children; we refuse to have major political discussions; we hate giving head—you know."

"Let's not talk about giving head," said Cleo. "Let's talk about dresses. I love talking about dresses."

"Here's what I think about dresses," said Rita. "Write this down: the study of clothes should be right up there with the study of nuclear physics, or possibly higher. The placement of a hemline, the tuck in a bodice, the thickness and nap of a fabric—all these things are riddled with meaning so deep and far-reaching that the findings would rock humankind if only someone would pay attention."

"That's what men think about the knuckleball," said Cleo, "only we don't get it. But we can look at a woman in a turquoise dress and figure where she bought it, why she bought it, what her house looks like, what books she reads, how often she has sex."

"She got it at Bolton's on Eighth Street," said Rita. "She bought it because she thought the shoulder pads would minimize her hips; she lives in Park Slope and her kitchen is done in daisy Con-Tac paper; she considers *Fear of Flying* a work of art; and she has sex twice a month with someone whose name is either Norman or Josh."

"No way," said Cleo. "His name is Eric. It's gotta be."

"My point is," said Rita, "clothes are as much of a science as baseball. But do men bring us popcorn and beer while we shop?"

"Actually, I *like* giving head," said Cleo out of nowhere.

"Let's not talk about giving head," I decided. "Let's talk about jealousy."

"Why can't we talk about giving head?" wondered Cleo pertly.

"Because I'll never forget your sperm-mask fiasco," I said cryptically.

"My last boyfriend before Herb," said Rita, "told me our relationship was ruined by an insistent subterranean hum of neurotic jealousy that emanated from my brain. And he was right. I am the jealous type. It started with my little brother. 'Would it be okay if I submerged his head in the toilet for about twenty minutes?' I remember asking my mother."

"The worst thing about jealousy," said Cleo, "is that you lose your sense of humor. Mel Brooks could come to dinner and a jealous person would only say, 'Pass the potatoes.'"

"I once hired a private detective to follow my husband around," piped up our waitress as she set a fresh round of drinks in front of us.

"Why?" we all asked.

"Well, he once told me something," she said as she sat down and lit a cigarette. "Oh, by the way, these drinks are on that fellow over there in the Burberry, the one talking to that girl in the turquoise dress. Someone should talk to her. Shoulder pads aren't everything.

"Anyway, once my husband said to me, 'Jenny, every man in the world wants to fuck every woman he can, and the only reason he doesn't is that his girlfriend or wife would eat him for breakfast.' I've never been the same."

"I think he was right," I said. "Men do have an overwhelming lust to conquer."

"Men have an overwhelming lust to lust; it's built into them biologically," said Cleo. "They want to put it everywhere. Let's talk about giving head."

"So we get jealous," said Rita, ignoring Cleo. "Who can blame us? We want to nest, they want to forage."

"I don't want to nest," I said.

"Yes you do, hon," said Jenny the waitress.

"I wasn't aware we'd met," I said coolly.

"No need to get huffy, doll," she said. "I see you in here with your boyfriend, the one who always wants to know exactly which river the trout comes from. Another girl looks at him, you look back daggers. Rightly so, too. He's gorgeous. Whoops! Well, I'd better get back to my other tables."

"I'll break her kneecaps," I said when she'd left.

"Permit me to interrupt," said the man in the Burberry, a bad penny. "Being an ex-reporter, I am also an inveterate eavesdropper, and I want to say you're wrong. Men may like to fuck around, but their jealousy, when aroused, is awesome. Actually, women only have two major flaws: They are manipulative and greedy."

General uproar.

"Hear me out," said the toad. "I'm a rich guy, wrote a magazine piece about a teenage heroin-addict transvestite that became a movie of the week. So every woman I go out with expects *cocaine*. Half of them angle for a car, the other half want a fur coat. I like to hang out in this dive, but if I don't take them to Lutèce they whimper. You women demand to be treated as equals, yet at the same time you want to be taken care of. This infuriates me."

"Well, I'm not like that," I said.

"Me neither," said Rita.

"You're the one who has been plying us with drink," said Cleo.

"Hey Fred!" someone called.

"Excuse me," said our new friend. "I'll be right back."

We looked at each other speculatively. "How rich do you think he is?" I asked.

"Do you think he has any cocaine on him at the moment?" wondered Cleo.

"Jesus, do you think he's right?" asked Rita.

We pondered silently for a moment. "Oh, what the hell, let's talk about jealousy again," I said.

JEALOUSY:
THE BIOLOGICAL IMPERATIVE

Worst thing in the world happened the other day. I was looking for a book and came across a secret cache of letters. Well, okay, *one* letter. The Kiwi was in England, thousands of miles away, and here was this letter I'd never seen before. Girlish handwriting. What to do?

I read the breezy little missive in a flash. Old girlfriend. Pining away for him. Lying in bed, eating salted nuts, drinking hibiscus tea, thinking about him.

Drinking hibiscus tea, thinking about him. The cow. The slut. The tramp. The tart. The troll.

I read the letter at approximately 1 A.M. By 2:30 it was clear I could never see him again—difficult since he lived with me, but not impossible. By 3:30 I realized I had no choice but to seek this woman out and ruin her life. By 5 A.M. they were both stone-cold dead, victims of a brutal bloodbath, and I was appearing at his funeral all in black, wearing an enigmatic smile behind my tasteful veil.

Ever have a fight transatlantically? Every well-chosen invective costs about $2.75. "If you're not home on the next flight you will not only never see me again but I will melt down your saxophones and dance on your guitars with hobnailed boots," I finally stated after $45 worth of strangled expletives and poisonous silences.

I was too enervated by my night of obsessive fury to round up the usual girlfriend network and spill the beans. My paranoia was baroque: I had, I figured, simply discovered the tip of the iceberg. Actually he was making it with every woman I had ever known or seen, maybe with men, maybe with dogs. When I tried to make breakfast I threw the toast across the room in a fit of frenzy. I took a Valium. Dissolved into tears. Finally called Cleo.

"I found this letter," I said.

"Come right over," she said.

A good girl, Cleo. She pointed out that there was a possibility, however slight, that I was overreacting.

"Give me a fucking break," I said. "How about the bit where she can't wait to feel his arms around her again?"

"*Again* is an extremely imprecise adverb," she advised. "And just remember, *she* wrote that letter, *he* didn't. She's obviously a silly bimbo and may well be harkening back to years ago. Believe me, this is a letter from a desperate hibiscus-tea drinker."

"She's going to be a lot more desperate after I've shoved a couple of knitting needles in her eyes."

Overreacting? *Moi?*

"Jesus Christ! *She* wrote the letter. *I* didn't. I can't control what she does." He was sitting in our living room, gray-skinned and shaking. Even the bags he had thrown into the doorway looked forlorn and frightened.

He denied everything.

I kept at him.

He kept denying.

At 6 A.M. he was crazed with jet lag and desperate for sleep. "Just tell me the truth," I said. "It will be all right. I won't mind. I just want to know."

"Well, we did do it once. I'm really sorry, you were out of town for a month. It was lust, plain and simple. Sowing the wild seed. It meant nothing. It's a relief to tell you, really. I've felt so guilty."

Immediately I kicked him in the stomach. "Get out of this house right now. You scumbag. Don't come back or you're a dead man."

There are two, count 'em, morals to this story:

1 Don't leave incriminating letters lying around.

2 Don't look for trouble.

These two morals are intertwined. A person who leaves letters around the house is down on his hands and knees groveling for trouble. Being a firm believer in the there-are-no-accidents school of life, I refuse to believe my lover accidentally left the particular bombshell where I might find it. I think things were going too smoothly. I think he wanted to stir things up, the passive-aggressive mouse.

But what kind of moronic impulse made me read it? I think things were going too smoothly. I think I wanted to stir things up—I'm a masochistic nit. We were colluding in this particular misery. It is of no use to anyone for me to know that he put a leg over this particular floozy. Except for torture value.

Here is a rule I have discovered too late: Do not feed paranoia. That means:

1 No sneaky reading of diaries.

2 NO GOING THROUGH DRAWERS.

3 NO COVERT MONITORING OF ANSWERING MACHINE MESSAGES.

4 NO STEAMING OPEN OF SUSPECT MAIL.

It is not only good manners to give one's lover his privacy, it is also in one's own self-interest. You know how your heart beats like a jackhammer in your chest when you do any of the above? It's the adrenaline pumping into your body because danger is lurking. Searching for infidelity is the most self-destructive practice in which one can indulge.

If you find something incriminating, you want to die. If you find nothing, you're totally flooded with self-revulsion for looking. Paranoia (read my lips) is nothing but self-punishment.

This is what I keep telling myself, over and over. It's not working.

He goes out for coffee, takes five minutes longer than expected, I'm suspicious. He comes home from band practice, takes a shower, I'm suspicious. He goes to work in the morning, I'm suspicious. He says he has a headache, I want him terminated.

"What can I do? I'm driving myself crazy," I said to Rita.

"You'll get over it in a couple of months," she said. "Sexual jealousy, contrary to what those nitwits in the sixties used to say—remember how they used to tell us we should all love each other and fuck everybody and not feel the teensiest bit possessive?—is a deep, primeval emotion. We all have it, sugar; it's built into our genes. It is a monster that lurks in our depths.

"Occasionally the monster surfaces, as when some imbecilic Kiwi leaves incriminating letters where paranoic girls can find them. And when the monster is stirred, it takes a while for him to subside. But he'll go away again, providing there isn't another incident."

"If there is, the man is dogmeat."

"If there is, he is history. If you don't kill him, I will. Any man who obliquely informs his girlfriend regularly that he is fucking around is beneath contempt. Once is horrible. Twice is unforgivable."

"So you think I should forgive him?"

"What the hell, give it a shot."

"You know the worst part, Rita? Not the infidelity; the betrayal. As horrible as it is to envision his body intermingled with another's, while she pants and squeals and he presses his—"

"You're not at all well."

"As bad as all that is, it is worse knowing he lied to me, kept a secret from me."

"Enough already," she snapped. "This man is not just an extension of you. He has his own life, his own problems. Of course he didn't tell you outright! This is life, darlin', not the soap opera of your dreams."

"Ah, well."

"Let it go, hon. You gotta trust them, even when you're not sure they're trustworthy. Trust them or leave them. Nothing else will work. Trust me."

GREAT EXPECTATIONS

Rented the movie *Arthur* again the other night. I just love *Arthur*. Dudley Moore: handsome, witty, rich, and drunk—sozzled because no one loves him. Falls madly in love with Liza Minelli, because she's kooky and steals ties for her father. Dudley is engaged to another, but he doesn't love her. He loves Liza, but she's a waitress; the family won't approve. I just love the way Dudley cackles in sudden glee. I just love the way he loves Liza.

Occasionally I think my life is Arthur-esque, like when I met Wendell. So funny, Wendell. I often fell over laughing. I liked his hair, I liked the way his face would go all innocent and deadpan right before he said something hilarious and then he would look surprised and start laughing at his own joke. I would go with him to nightclubs where once in a while he would break into a dance that made him look like a flower swaying in the wind. "Pretend I'm wearing a muumuu," Wendell would say. He is perfect; he is even English.

So Wendell had a girlfriend. But he never mentioned her and hardly ever saw her; she was clearly a convenience. He drank to excess. One night, when it was very late and we were sitting in a beautiful nightclub with chandeliers and candles glittering and a starlet with a sequined dress was passed out at our table, Wendell leaned very close to me, so that our cheekbones were touching, and said with pure love gleaming in his eyes, "You're the one for me. You're just the one I want." I nodded, brimming with sweetness, and put my head on his shoulder. His girlfriend was around somewhere, talking to a rock musician, but that wasn't important.

Later Wendell pulled me into a secluded alcove and we kissed for several deeply passionate minutes. It was a dream come true.

Another big favorite of mine is *His Girl Friday*. I ache with joy at the way Cary Grant and Rosalind Russell snap scorching remarks at each other faster than the ear can hear, each one topping the other with Machiavellian antics, feints, and counterfeints. Of course Rosalind doesn't marry stodgy Ralph Bellamy! Of course she goes back to Cary, who really loves her!

Once there was a man I really loved: Rex. He looked a bit like Cary Grant, actually. I remember that when I first met him, on the street, he was with a good friend of mine and they said, "Come to dinner with us at the Cuban joint around the corner."

Now, the reason I was walking down the street at all was that I was meeting Rita at the Lion's Head for drinks, but when I saw Rex, my other engagement went clean out of my head. I forgot everything; the world stopped. I went with him to the Cuban joint. I went with him everywhere for the next few months; we were enmeshed in a dizzying love affair, full of passion and fights and magic nights.

He promised to buy me a dress once. We had a major falling-out. Furious, I sent him a telegram saying, "It's all over between us. Please send dress." He cabled back: "What size?"

Then out of nowhere he packed his things and moved to Los Angeles to write screenplays.

I was miserable, but I loved him and therefore knew it would work out. I called him late one night, said I couldn't go another day without seeing him and would be arriving on the next plane.

Which I did. Rex was waiting, with roses. We kissed and he scooped up my bags and led me into the longest, whitest limousine I had ever seen, which he had supplied with iced champagne and which he couldn't possibly afford, just like I couldn't afford the airfare. We kissed again as we sped through the night.

I will always adore the movie *Who'll Stop the Rain?* Nick Nolte's character is a dream man—strong, wild, and gritty, saying things like, "I'm tired of taking shit from inferior people." He falls in love with Tuesday Weld, who's hooked on pills and then on heroin, and he fights to his death to save her. "She's the love of my life," he says, and you can see his pain and vulnerability.

The love of my life was a man I'll call Luke, and he was around during my drug period. I had a brief flurry when I would snort cocaine and swallow Quaaludes and have a nap in my dinner. Luke would hold me, he would take care of me and drive me to supermarkets at four in the morning. For some reason I felt safe in supermarkets. He was tough and funny, but he always had this pain in his eyes. I was the only one who understood him, the only one he could talk to. Sometimes he would say, "I love you, I love you," again and again.

My latest love affair is basically Annie Hall in reverse. I'm Woody Allen; he is young and beautiful and doesn't mind Hollywood. I try to turn him into me, wanting him to read my favorite books and enjoy my favorite movies. He can't get over how neurotic and intractable I can be or how long I have been in therapy.

I remember once sitting on an airplane with him and thinking, "What am I doing with this man? We have no future." And I looked at him and could tell he was thinking the same thing about me, and my heart lurched with a dreadful fear. Then I could see the same fear in his eyes, and we fell into each other's arms and clung to each other for the rest of the journey.

So here's what happened with me and Wendell: Nothing. We never kissed again. No allusion was ever made to that fateful night. He is still with his girlfriend. Maybe always will be. We are friends again, but it will always be a little weird.

Here's what happened with me and Rex: He just got married to a film editor in L.A. Writing that first screenplay made him all nervous and edgy and things never jelled between us. A year later he took me out to dinner and then wanted to go home with me, but he was living with someone else and so was I; it didn't seem right.

Here's what happened with me and Luke: He said he couldn't make a commitment! The old chestnut. I didn't believe him and plagued him with amusing postcards and amorous letters; once I even tried to abduct him. Now if I ever see him, we are very formal and polite.

Here's what is still happening with me and the Kiwi: We drive each other within inches of distraction. We decide to break up and then realize we just can't.

Sometimes we torture each other; we're good at that. Sometimes we fall into bed, another strong skill. Nothing is resolved.

Here's what I really want: I want a life directed by George Cukor and scripted by William Goldman. I want Ry Cooder to do the score, Edith Head the costumes. I want quick edits, good lighting, snappy dialogue.

I always fully expect that my life will turn out like the movies, but my life has remained recalcitrant. It forever disappoints me. I keep expecting that enormous, monumental kiss and the swell of music and the final fade to wonderfulness.

Whenever I see one of my favorite movies I cry at the end—but not those fun, happy-ending tears; tears of rage and frustration. I just don't understand.

Why can't I live happily ever after? What am I doing wrong?

OTHER PEOPLE

THE DEPARTMENT OF DEPORTATION

It seems to me, correct me if I'm wrong, that there are an awful lot of people in Manhattan. And it's getting worse.

I am in the habit of having a nice, peaceful, grumpy breakfast with my ex-boyfriend and now buddy Jake at our local eatery on Seventh Avenue. We try to get there by 11 A.M., an admirable feat for two sleepyheads who would rather never get up at all, in order to beat the noon rush of riffraff, who would ruin our digestion.

But lately many inappropriate people, some wearing jumpsuits, have been pouring in earlier and earlier and sitting at tables adjacent to ours, where they proceed to talk about things. Job interviews, tofu recipes, relationship intricacies, and expense accounts are topics discussed with enervating relish within shot of our delicate ears.

I want these people out of my sight. Actually I usually want to shoot them, but one must be fair. Everyone who wants to should be allowed to live. But that does not mean that they should be allowed to live in Manhattan, busily driving up apartment prices, taking every parking space, and forming huge lines in front of me at movie theaters. Let's face it: Deportation is the only way.

A Department of Deportation must be established

immediately, and I would like to propose Jake and me as the entire board of directors. I know for sure that we would do the right thing—we are both sober, simple, responsible human beings without one shred of viciousness. Not one welfare mother need shrink from our steely gaze; only the pretentious and/or malevolent need cower.

Just think: a city without makeup salesgirls and flinty-eyed landlords! A city free of French maitre d's and publicists! No more joggers, Scientologists, Aesthetic Realists, video artists, lawyers, mimes! No New Jersey drivers!

"How will we keep them out?" Jake wondered.

"Simple," I said. "We round up all the doorpeople from all the nightclubs and triple their salaries if only they will guard the entrances to the Lincoln, Holland, and Midtown tunnels and to all bridges. Not only will anyone wishing to come into Manhattan have to pay a large admission fee, but they will also have to be 'on the list.' Not only will they have to be on the list, they'll have to be wearing quietly tasteful clothes, have clean hair, and not be wearing designer sunglasses."

"We'll have to keep a firm watch on airports, trains, and bus stations," decided Jake, warming to the theme.

"They'll have to apply for admission three months in advance."

"Absolutely three months. What the hell, let's make it six. And they'll need three references from Manhattan residents, which will then be carefully vetted by us."

"Also everyone now residing in Manhattan must come under review," I said. "That man at the next table, for example, is wearing an orange cable-knit sweater. He's out of here."

"Those guys who lurk at department store escalators and try to throw perfume on you," said Jake.

"All men with shoulder bags," I said.

"Ladies in mink coats who clog Soho on Sundays."

"Trendy florists who put decent luncheonette owners out of business."

"Purveyors of nouvelle cuisine."

"Psychiatric social workers."

"Men with beards."

"Men with beards?" asked Jake. "Who do you think
you are?"

"Okay, Jake, not you," I said hastily. "You can stay.
I like your beard. I have fond memories of your beard.
But as a rule, I detest facial foliage. So many men
who cultivate a beard will go that crucial next step and
begin to affect a pipe, not to mention sports jackets
with leather elbow patches."

"If men with beards go," said Jake with a dangerous
glint in his eye, "so do all women who wear shoulder
pads."

"How can you say this?" I wailed. "Have you lost
your mind? Do you want me to walk around looking
like the Goodyear blimp? Shoulder pads are crucial to
my well-being!"

"No beards, no shoulder pads," said Jake equably.

Readers, we've decided to let everyone stay. But
please, if you happen to enter a coffee shop on Seventh
Avenue in the late morning and notice a bearded fellow
drinking coffee with a girl wearing giant shoulder pads,
take a table as far away from them as possible. And
please don't laugh at them.

DUTIES OF A GUEST

The moment Daylight Savings Time is upon us or
the Christmas season rears its spangled head, most of
us become frantic. We know that now is the time to
cast our keening minds toward that happy day when
some poor benighted soul will rescue us from steamy
streets or family dinners by inviting us out to her coun-

try home for a few days. We grovel shamelessly, hint blatantly for such invites. Usually we manage to cadge one or two.

But be advised that one cannot simply stuff one's overnight bag and trip off without a care in the world. One must, in order to be a more perfect guest, take one's hosts into regard. One must realize that hosts are sensitive flowers with hopes and dreams and needs, and if one wants to be invited back, one had better be alive to their every whim. Just follow these simple rules:

1 REMEMBER THAT ONE'S HOSTS ARE IN-SECURE They want to please and entertain you, but they just don't know *how*.

"What the hell are we going to do with them all weekend?" you'll find many a beleaguered host saying to her equally confused husband.

"Possibly we should take them fishing?" this husband will suggest cautiously, thereby causing his wife to tear at her hair in dismay. Suggestions of bridge-playing, charades, and taffy-pulling will be similarly dispatched.

You simply must assuage your host's fears by taking the entertainment question into your own hands.

For example, every host loves a surprise.

Suppose, just for fun, you arrive not only bearing an overnight bag but an exotic foreign gentleman as well! Your host will gasp with astonishment, but rest assured she will be thrilled to the marrow if you happen to have in tow a mysterious Lebanese fellow who, although he speaks little English, is extremely charismatic on the subject of modern firearms. And if the mysterious gentleman also happens to be carrying under his arm a slide projector bearing slides of his bucolic native land, so much the better! Many hours of merry entertainment will be thus taken care of.

2 REMEMBER THAT NO HOST IS AN ISLAND   We are, in fact, our host's keeper, and many a host is, in his or her own way, crying out for psychological guidance.

Say, for instance, that the first course of a delightful dinner has been consumed and your host reaches for a pack of cigarettes. The thoughtful guest will immediately slap the host's hand and exclaim brightly, "Now, now! You know that cigarette smoking is a poisonous and filthy habit. We'll just take these right now, shall we?" Then immediately march into the bathroom and flush the entire pack down the toilet. Your host will thank you in the end.

A similar fate should befall any drugs that happen to surface. Should your host offer you a hit of a reefer, pour linseed oil over his entire supply. Should he proffer cocaine on a mirror, blow it back into his face with a hearty chuckle. Be really altruistic and drink all his fifty-year-old port yourself.

3 BE CHEERFUL IN THE MORNING   No host likes to be confronted with a grumpy slugabed of a guest who, when he finally emerges from his bedroom at 10 A.M., says good morning and leaves it at that.

Country folk arise with the chickens, and nothing warms their hearts so much as guests who do likewise.

So spring out of bed at 7 A.M., inhale a lungful of fresh, uncluttered air, and burst into song. If no melody occurs, it is permissible to practice your scales. Or, even better, play a musical instrument, like the tuba.

If your host doesn't emerge from her bedroom after the first three minutes, she is simply signaling to you that she desires your presence. Enter uproariously. If she and her husband happen to have pillows pulled over their heads, pull them right off. Then tickle your hosts' feet with a handy feather and tease them about their lazy ways. This will put them in a festive mood.

4 BRING YOUR OWN ACCESSORIES   A host naturally has many things on her mind and may
simply have forgotten some trifling matter like food.
Best to come prepared with copious amounts of sea-
weed, wheat germ, brewer's yeast, and blackstrap
molasses, which, as we all know, are the four wonder-
foods that country types crave. Bring pots and pans as
well. Insist on doing all the cooking. But leave the
washing up, or your host will have nothing to do and
feel guilty.

5 MAKE FRIENDS WITH THE CHILDREN   Many
hosts have been blessed with issue. It will be
incumbent upon you to make friends with the little
folk. Bring along a pleasant gift—a toy drum kit or a
BB gun are always greeted with cries of delight by our
young friends.

Parents are often loath to discipline their offspring
when guests are present; show you care by doing it for
them. If little Phoebe hits you smartly on the nose
with a rubber band, *you* give her the spanking she
needs. If a screaming temper tantrum ensues, explain
carefully that little girls who cry are invariably eaten
that same night by hungry tigers escaped from nearby
zoos. She will then behave prettily.

As an added bonus, tell any children you happen
to meet the facts of life. Often your hosts will not have
gotten around to this grisly duty, and their gratitude
will be boundless.

6 STAY FOREVER   Hosts get lonely, hosts get blue,
hosts need peppy people around them to brighten
the day. If they ask you to come on Friday and leave
on Sunday, pay no attention and stay three weeks.
They secretly want you to.

And that's it. Follow these instructions to the letter,
and I should do very well for myself this summer.

PARENTING MADE EASY

About five years ago it was impossible to venture out of one's house without running into great clots of women discussing men, relationships, and sex. Topics included were (a) Why he hadn't called, (b) Why, even though he had called, he was still a jerk, (c) Why he was pretending to be afraid of commitment, and (d) All of the above. One couldn't avoid these pervasive agonizings; they were the meat and potatoes of all feminine social intercourse.

But there has been a great upheaval! Somehow most of these women have been pinned down by the men of their dreams and are married, and can now speak of nothing else but babies.

Whether to have one. Whether one is too old to have one. Whether one needs nursery school or a housekeeper. The pros and cons of amniocentesis, sonograms, breast-feeding, natural childbirth. Coping with parenthood and careers.

And to completely solidify the trend, there is even a baby backlash. Several prominent magazines seem to feel the necessity of publishing cold blasts of anti-parenthood sentiment: Parents are boring, parents are self- and baby-absorbed, parents become more bovine than any self-respecting cow would ever be.

What's the truth? Does becoming a parent release some exotic brain enzyme that turns one immediately tedious? Or is parenthood, in fact, the most deeply moving and fulfilling experience of life? Should all women stop pushing the snooze alarms of their biological clocks and get on with it? Or what?

The truth is that all new parents are wildly boring. They have to be—it's their only defense against madness.

I went to a baby shower last year, an occurrence that has been indelibly branded on my brain pan. All women. All movers and shakers in chosen careers. Everybody had a hundred-dollar haircut. Shrimp was served.

One woman discussed her movie deal, another spoke in glowing terms of her advertising budget. The prospective mom, eight months pregnant, told us how she was just finishing her novel. Then the presents were opened and everyone squealed over the yellow booties and pastel afghans. Everybody said she wanted to be a mother as soon as possible; everybody also said she would never descend to talking about it.

"After all," said the hostess brightly, "nobody wants to listen to somebody talking about teething or diapers or colic. Cynthia, you're the only actual mother here. You never talked about *teething*, did you?"

"Well," I said, "I did mention teething once or twice, yes. In fact I talked of nothing else for months on end. Even the postman started avoiding me."

"Oh ha ha ha, Cynthia, what a card you are." They all laughed.

Card, hey? Perhaps I should have told them about the nursing mothers' group I joined, at which we were often gripped for hours over which emollient would best care for cracked nipples. Perhaps do a replay of myself on the diaper-service-versus-disposables question. Maybe they should meet some of my friends whom I used to turn glassy-eyed and staring at their watches by relentless delving into cradle cap.

Yes, I was boring! I was shell-shocked, I was crazed. I was exhausted. I was stricken with cabin fever, culture shock, postpartum depression. I was an utter, total, irretrievable wreck. Motherhood had brought me to my knees.

At the time, I never told anybody. No way, José. Other people coped; other people were fine. Other people were placid and adored parenthood. Floundering about in my miasma of grisly confusion, the topic of teething would spring to mind.

Teething! I could talk about that! I knew all about it! Coherent sentences could be formed!

After six months of no sleep, of my life turning into an updated version of Dante's inferno, and yet still feeling a deep, abiding, perpetual, and abject love for my heavenly baby, *boring* was not an epithet, it was an aspiration.

You don't believe me. Motherhood will be different for you. This is what I always thought! I would be the new, groovy mom with backpack full of baby, singing a merry melody while I tramped through my jolly life with my fun baby-accessory.

Now I'm seeing that same pathetic, drawn, shaken, and confused look in the eyes of my friends who have just become parents. They can't believe nobody told them the truth. Here it is:

Motherhood is all it's cracked up to be, and more. The first month you're so tired you will bump into walls. The idea of a full night's sleep, even an uninterrupted nap, will become a vague and receding dream. Plus your hormones are hitting you with a triple whammy, kind of as if PMS were magnified a hundred times. Then your baby will invariably contract some benign rash on his cheek and you, owing to sleep-deprived hysteria and rampant hormonal imbalance, will be positive he has developed at least leprosy.

But this is just the first year. Then it gets easier and more amusing. Here is a brief outline of highlights you will encounter afterward:

THE ONE-YEAR-OLD He has learned to walk, he has learned to wave bye-bye and say *mama* and *ball*. Your time will be divided equally between changing diapers, having your heart stop because you realize he hasn't been in the room with you for two full minutes and he has undoubtedly stuck his finger in a light socket or emptied all the detergent onto the floor,

cultivating other parents with one-year-olds with whom
you discuss play groups, wishing you had seen one of
the movies nominated for an Academy Award, and
praying fiercely for a decent baby-sitter.

THE TWO-YEAR-OLD   Has learned to run and un-
latch child-proof locks. Has temper tantrums. Says
"No!" at every possible moment. Throws all his food
on the floor. Wants a puppy. You will constantly be
trying to get him to stay in his stroller, changing diapers, taking him to playgroups only to have him dis-
solve into inconsolable sobbing when you try to leave,
tripping over building blocks, crushing crayons beneath your feet, and praying fiercely for a decent baby-
sitter.

THE THREE-YEAR-OLD   Likes to chat. Must speak
to everyone who calls on the phone. Is obsessed with
"Sesame Street." Refuses to bathe. Must have twelve
bedtime stories read to him before he can fall asleep.
Constantly needs a drink of water. Is positive he can
drive a car. You will mainly be changing his clothes
because of his many toilet-training accidents, remem-
bering how to finger-paint, explaining why he can't
have a puppy, supervising five other three-year-olds on
"your day," having the odd friend for dinner and ab-
sentmindedly cutting her meat for her, and praying
fiercely that your baby-sitter doesn't leave town.

THE FOUR-YEAR-OLD   Has a constant runny nose.
Can only sleep if five stuffed animals are tucked in
neatly beside him. Is bored with nursery school, thinks
he's too grown up for those other "babies." Says "fuck
you, motherfucker" and trills delightedly when your
face turns puce. You will spend all your time finding
his shoes and buying his baby-sitter many gifts so she
doesn't leave you.

THE FIVE-YEAR-OLD   Thinks he is a grown-up, only
smaller. Wants to write television sit-coms. Will not
wear certain clothes to kindergarten, claiming they are
tacky. Is vastly offended by not being allowed to cross

the street by himself. Falls in love with alarming abandon. Your life will be punctuated by parent-teacher
conferences, dissuading your child from wearing his
toy gun and holster to school, finding his lost teddy
bear, explaining why the tooth fairy only left a quarter
when she left Eric a five-dollar bill, and praying fiercely
for another baby-sitter.

After the first five years your child will be so convinced he is an adult that you will start believing him,
especially when he starts bringing home report cards.
Report cards, more than anything else, remind us
powerfully of the rigors and fears and dizzying dreams
of childhood and, although we had until this time
loved our child with such a fierce passion that we could
get dizzy with the emotion, that first report card brings
with it the most binding emotion of all: empathy.

COSMIC TYPECASTING

"Jesus, Mahatma, is that you? You scared me out
of my wits."

It is not often you walk into your own living room,
fresh from the horrors of Christmas shopping, to encounter a small man with flowing beard and impeccably tailored robes prancing underneath the weight
of an enormous bouquet of holly.

"It is I, here in all my wonderment. Mahatma
Grossman, Holy Man, at your service. Season's greet-
ings. I have brought you holly."

Why do I need a Holy Man in my life? I wondered
fitfully as Mahatma began thrusting holly into every
available orifice of my living room. Ever since that
day I met him on Fourteenth Street, he persists in
manifesting himself, plaguing my existence with his

cosmic wisdom. He says I am his favorite disciple. It is impossible to dissuade him.

"Today we will talk about cosmic types," said Mahatma.

"Why?"

"Because I wish it. More and more cosmic types are infesting the country. Many of them are not sincere; some are even dangerous and unpleasant. Your readers need to know the facts. Bring out your little notebook, and is it possible you have a beer for a parched Holy Man? Those are very nice shoes you're wearing."

Mahatma sat in my favorite chair and fussily rearranged his robes. When his beer arrived he chugged it quickly, wiped his mouth, and thundered, "Beware the cosmic businessman!"

"Huh?"

"He will rip off your face and make a terrine of your entrails. He will steal your house, your car, your job, your lover. If you find a man in a pinstriped business suit who has either a guru or a psychic healer, run for your life. He is evilness incarnate!"

"You mean like that guy I used to know who worked for the advertising agency and told me it was bad karma that slaughtered all those Jews in the Holocaust? I always wondered about him."

"He is *mal de tête!* He is *stúpido!*"

"So multilingual, Mahatma!"

"He is a fascist pigface! You see how it works: The poor are poor because of their second-rate karma. Abused children were executioners in a former life. Cripples? They are all reincarnations of murderers and rapists. The poor souls your cosmic businessman has screwed out of their last pennies? In a past life they were theatrical agents. Thus does your cosmic businessman rationalize his ruthless behavior! He has no guilt! By his system, every form of perfidy is permitted! Destroy him if you can!"

"Speaking of which, Mahatma, do you think that God is a right-wing supremacist? He seems to be killing off third-world people with reckless abandon, what with volcanos and earthquakes and famine. And now he's got it in for homosexuals, junkies, Africans, and Haitians. Is this a plot?"

"We shall not concern ourselves with God at the moment. By the way, that blouse you're wearing is truly obscene. Where did you get it?"

"Betsey Johnson."

"Another slut, one can only assume. *Beware the cosmic hippie!*"

"Pardon?"

"He has long, unwashed hair and wears an unpleasant leather hat, stitched with rawhide. He tucks his corduroy jeans into his hideously elfin boots. He writes books about dolphins who speak in tongues. He takes drugs and is all arrogance, speaking with a sneer of 'straight people.' His sense of humor is flaccid, his cosmicity is his crutch. He desires and needs all other humans to feel inferior to him. He only laughs at others' expense. He wants power and collects misguided acolytes, into whom he pumps psychedelics. His beatific smile belies an ego as big as the Ritz. He suffers from sexual incontinence. Shun him." Mahatma belched happily.

"You mean like that woman who once tried to steal my boyfriend?" I asked. "She was wearing a black diaphanous dress that had little mirrors all over it. She whispered throatily to him about the tantric secrets she had in her fingertips."

"No, no! You know nothing! Here, I've brought you some mistletoe. But don't kiss me. I prefer Spanish weightlifters."

"Some Holy Man."

"I work in mysterious ways, my wonders to perform. The she-devil you allude to is the cosmic Kim Novak clone. She saw *Bell, Book and Candle* as an impressionable child. She hums mystic tunes. She has a cat named Piewacket. She believes herself a mysterious seductress. She hates other women."

"Why?"

"She is a woman with disgust of her own sex. She is cold and manipulative and unfeeling. She reads palms and wants to go into the essential oils business. Cut her on the street."

"But pray tell, oh Holy Man, are there no good cosmic people?"

"Why yes, dozens. I am one. A good cosmic soul is not using metaphysics to hide personal inadequacies, hidden hostility, or selfish pyrotechnics. He is full of the pain and suffering of humanity, yet tries to transcend whatever he can. He throws himself into lost causes. He is humble; he knows he is the biggest fool who ever existed. He will watch "Bloopers and Practical Jokes" on television and not sneer. He will pull out his tarot cards at parties, but then he will put them away and dance the hootchie-koo. He makes no judgments."

"Makes no judgments, Mahatma my sweet?"

"Bring me another beer, you misbegotten minx!"

He poured the beer down his throat and then, as is his wont, disappeared in a cloud of smoke.

WHAT ARE FRIENDS FOR?

MONDAY

Terror, desolation, shock, stupor, tears, bloodcurdling grief, apocalyptic fury. He's done the one thing that cannot be forgiven, smoothed over, laughed at. A drawn-out scene of violent psychological damage erupts in the bedroom. The kid lurks politely in the living room, then decides the really gentlemanly thing to do is pop out to the store for a magazine and some gum.

"Please leave now," I say to my lover.

"Is this it then?" he says back.

"Yes. Good-bye," I say.

"Good-bye," he says.

A few minutes later the kid returns, looks at me, goes to bed in confusion. I sit and stare until the phone rings. It is Herb, saying he just got a lead role on Broadway. Praise the lord.

TUESDAY

I wake up, remember, and cry. My pink princess phone first puts me in touch with Cleo, who's giggling. Zeke just came back into her life, he is there, they've just had a shower. "But I detect a certain tear-stained quality to your voice," she says. "What's up?"

"Call me back when he leaves," I say. "And he will be leaving, never fear."

"Huh?" she says as call waiting bleeps. Rita. She's tense, big job today. "But what's wrong, sugar? Tell me quick."

"Later," I say. "Good luck, break a leg." I dial the phone. "Lucy?"

"Hello, you silly old tart. How are you?"

"Oh, Lucy."

"Let me guess. It's that bloody Kiwi, isn't it? I told you to have no truck with Colonials, but did you listen? What's he done?"

"It doesn't even matter what he's done."

"My God, he's gone?"

"He's in the past."

"Sure?"

"Sure as I'm born."

"Ah. Well then, meet me in an hour at Seventy-fifth and Broadway."

"Don't be ridiculous."

"Be there. You will be attending ballet class. Don't say no. It will be best. You won't have time to think."

"Fine," I sniffle. And hang up to put on clothes and apply shaky blusher. The phone rings; it is Rita.

"Just tell me, is it the Kiwi?"

"Yes."

"I knew it! I'll call you later. 'Bye."

At Seventy-fourth and Broadway I realize I've forgotten to eat. Lucy is waiting for me with a quart of iced coffee and a buttered roll. "Eat this, drink this," she says, "and then we'll go upstairs and get you ballet slippers."

She sits me down while a salesman pushes pink leather shoes on my boatlike feet. Finally she can contain herself no longer. "Guess what?" she says. "I got two calls from casting agents!"

"Terrific," I say. "And casting agents never break your heart. Oh, and guess what else—Herb got the part on Broadway."

"Oh I hate him, I hate him!" she shrieks.

"And Cleo seems to be back with Zeke."

"She's mentally ill. Now, directly after class I will arrange to have your erstwhile boyfriend's things removed from your apartment."

"No!"

"Yes. You can't do it. It will make you too sad."

The ballet teacher has been apprised discreetly of my position. He is terribly supportive as my foot teeters in shaky arcs, whereas he testily calls his other students "little Martha Graham Crackers."

"Rita called, Cleo called, Herb called, Grandma called, Jake called, Adam called and said he'd be here at five o'clock," the kid says, his eyes glued to MTV, when I get home. "And I'll need a bicycle helmet before Grandma and Grandpa take me on the bicycle trip. And how are you feeling?"

"Please, can we listen to George Jones?" I ask.

"Just this once," the dream-child answers.

Meanwhile Cleo and Rita are chatting on the phone. "Now every woman in the world will be after Herb," Rita is saying.

"I never did like that vile Kiwi," Cleo is saying.

At home I am putting new gray cotton sheets on the sofa bed for Adam, my house guest for a week, visiting from England, assigning stories for his magazine. Jake is in the other room, packing the Kiwi's things with unseemly relish.

"Lucy told me to come on over," Jake says when I look at him askance.

"I just don't want to hear any words of wisdom," I say.

"I brought some Wild Turkey boxes from my favorite liquor store," he says.

Adam arrives at five, exhausted. "So wonderful to see you," I say, hugging him.

"What's Cleo doing tonight, do you know?" asks Adam. "I'm determined to get her back. And how are you?"

I tell him and he immediately offers to make a cup of tea.

"Better make it a vat of margaritas," says the kid.

"I'll drink to that," mutters Jake as he packs the last box.

WEDNESDAY

"Okay, we've got something really serious here," Rita says as I pick up the phone, "so pull yourself together. Neville is very sick. He collapsed last night. He's in the hospital, something to do with a kidney. We may need to find the best doctor in the world."

"Where's Lucy?"

"Where a wife should be. By his side. I'm on my way over there."

"Shall I come?"

"No, you find a doctor. Call someone who knows."

The phone rings. Cleo. "Well," she says, "are we holding up? Are we suicidal? Shall I bring over some Hank Williams tapes?"

"Never mind that," I say. "First we have to find a doctor for Neville."

The phone rings. "This is the exterminator," a voice says, "reminding you of your appointment tomorrow morning. Don't forget to empty all your kitchen cupboards."

The phone rings. "Is Brodie all ready for his trip on Sunday?" his grandmother asks.

The phone rings. "You don't perchance know where Neville is?" wonders Adam. "I'm supposed to meet him here and he's really late. I need to collect those articles from him today. It's urgent."

"Adam dear, perhaps you'd better sit down," I say.

Phones ring all over the city as Herb, Cleo, Adam, Jake, Rita, and I get Neville the best doctor in the world. Lucy is fed Cleo's Valium. Rita finishes her big job and then calls Lucy's casting agent. Adam deals with jet lag and pleads with Cleo to no avail. I leave home while the Kiwi comes to collect the boxes, but manage to arrive before he is finished. He is in tears. I am in tears. Adam is drinking a cup of tea. The Kiwi leaves. The kid hugs me. Rita arrives with a joint and a bottle of tequila. "Drink," she says, "smoke." She adds, "Neville is probably okay."

THURSDAY

"That's about it," says Cleo as we finish emptying the last kitchen cupboard.

"Perhaps we should have a nice cup of tea," says Adam.

"Mom, don't forget the bicycle helmet," the kid says.

"I told Herb and Rita we'd meet them for a celebratory lunch," Cleo says, avoiding Adam's eye.

The phone rings. "My apartment's been burgled!" shouts Jake.

SOCIAL WEIRDNESS

As a public service, I have assembled a panel of the finest minds in the country to answer the common yet sticky social problems that plague many humans in their quest for peace and harmony.

The members of the panel are so high-minded that they prefer to remain anonymous, since any kind of publicity is repellent to them.

("Ha ha ha," says Mahatma.

"Ho ho ho," says Rita.

"Who's she kidding?" asks Neville.)

Ahem. We shall just call them the Social Arbiters.

■

Dear Social Arbiters:

My girlfriend is screenplay-mad. She's sure she's about to make a million dollars any day now by writing a hit movie that she figures will star Eddie Murphy. I have no problem with this as a concept, but my girlfriend has become the most tedious person on earth.

She wakes up in the morning and tells me her dreams—involved, murky, pointless meanderings that would no doubt make any shrink shriek with joy but always leave me feeling as if I'd just swallowed a lump of cold oatmeal. Here's an example:

She's married and she has a child and then she isn't married anymore and she's living in Connecticut but then she's on "Family Feud" and then she's home again but she hears someone crying and calls the police but the police aren't interested but she keeps calling and calling and finally gets them interested but it's a different policeman not the first one and anyway there's a little boy hiding in another apartment that has no kitchen.

"Isn't that exciting, honey?" she'll say to me. "And when the camera panned to the last shot with the boy sobbing, I knew I had it."

"Had what?" I ask.

"Why, the entire screenplay."

"Wait, hang on, weren't we discussing your dream last night? Did I get lost somewhere?"

"Sure, but wouldn't it make a dynamite screenplay?"

You see what I'm up against. My girlfriend isn't even a writer. She breeds horses for a living. One day she was a normal person, the next day this. It's been months now. How can I stop her?

Harvey P.

Dear Harvey:

Think back. Immediately before your g.f. started displaying these disquieting symptoms, did you have a friend return from Los Angeles? And did you have this friend over for dinner? And sometime during this dinner, did your friend take both your girlfriend's hands in his, look her in the eyes, and say, "Good to see you, Gladys, really"?

Reflect and you will realize that this has happened. What you don't realize is this: When your friend took your girlfriend's hand in his and threw her some heavy eye contact, *he was passing along the dread screenplay virus.*

The screenplay virus is a pesky little devil that scientists finally isolated in a small pond in Topanga Canyon, where some irresponsible hippie with no karma to speak of dumped a large amount of acid that had been contaminated that morning at the Polo Lounge when Swifty Lazar sneezed on it.

The symptoms are simple: The afflicted are absolutely convinced they have at least a "Movie of the Week" in them. Their speech becomes riddled with such phrases as "take a meeting" and "let's have lunch." If not restrained, they will go out and buy a license plate that says GO FR IT.

You cannot cure your beloved, but you can see that she is comfortable. Listen to her ravings, nod pleasantly, and say things like "Yes darling, that sounds like a perfect vehicle for Dusty Hoffman." Make sure she gets plenty of liquids and bed rest.

And this is crucial: Keep her out of the sun. This disease is often fatal for the suntanned.

Social Arbiters

■

Dear Social Arbiters:

I didn't mean to eavesdrop. I was just minding my own business. But I left my portfolio behind so I had to go back. That's when I heard everything.

"I don't think she's brainless at all," Lorraine was saying to Phil. "She's nice and funny and bright. I like her. And I think it's very crude of you to say you just feel like fucking her occasionally and calling her a bimbo. You're a pig."

I couldn't imagine who they were talking about. I just stood there in the hall, wondering. Then Phil spoke. "I'm not such a pig," he said. "I've let her stay here for two weeks without paying rent, haven't I?"

Me! He was talking about me! The pig. I've cooked! Cleaned! Sewed buttons on his stupid ugly Yohji Yamamoto shirts! Bought the groceries, picked up the laundry! Waxed the floor! Scraped years of grease off the kitchen window! The foul fool!

I never, not once, slept with him. I might have but he said he wasn't into sex. Thank God.

I want to kill him.

I can't kill him, I'm such a wimp. I just left immediately. But I feel the need for slow, icy revenge. Yet I've always been taught that revenge is evil. What are your views? Can you think of anything really juicy?

Wronged Woman

P.S. He says he's an ex-hippie but he works for an advertising agency.

Dear Wronged:

We are pleased you mentioned the advertising aspect; otherwise we might have spent days biting our fingernails and staring off into space trying to come up with the perfect revenge scenario.

But luckily advertising will do your dirty work. Even as you read this, the man's soul is turning to dust. Any ideas he once held have soured, any self-respect shriveled, any integrity shot to hell.

As soon as the God-monster advertising starts doling you a weekly paycheck, you are no longer a human being but a mere sniveling cog, ready to sell your mother if only the client will like the story boards. Advertising takes no prisoners; it turns your blood to liquid greed and your brain to gelatinous paranoia. You may start out an innocent ex-hippie trying to make ends meet in clean blue jeans, but will inevitably end up wearing awful two-toned shoes with tassles on them. (We are not discussing here all people concerned with advertising, but simply those who work for those huge agencies.)

Do not worry. You need do nothing. This poor man is transforming himself into a crawly beast without any help from you.

Although if you were suddenly overcome with

the desire to write all your single friends (both sexes) postcards saying, "Oh, by the way, did I ever tell you that Phil's penis is three inches long?" these social arbiters wouldn't try to stop you.

Social Arbiters

■

Dear Social Arbiters:

I've got a couple across my courtyard who fight. She screeches, he whines in a rumbly sort of way. They're at it at least twice a week. Listening to them makes me crazy, especially since the acoustics in the courtyard preclude me from actually hearing what they're saying. All that comes across is "screech screech!"

"Whine!"

"Screech, screech, screech!"

"Whine, whine!"

It's not enough to keep the mind alive. Is there a way to stop them?

Roger

Dear Roger:

Next time you pass one of them at the mailbox, say something like, "Great one you had last night! Really enjoyable. I was on your side totally. Although I did think she had you there for a while."

They'll get soundproofing immediately.

Social Arbiters

■

Dear Social Arbiters:

What about the breast question? Marlene and I are thinking of going topless this summer. Matter of fact, Marlene already has. I happened to glance her way and there were her jugs, looking like an order of poached eggs winking at the sun.

"Won't they burn, Marlene?" I queried from the swimming pool (we have rented one of those

summer houses that cost a million dollars a month).

"I've got them covered," Marlene said. "I've put fifteen on the actual nipples, then on that supersensitive area about two inches in diameter just surrounding the areola I've slathered eight, which I've blended in very nicely with my usual four to achieve that radiant glow of pure sun-kissed health."

"Ah, well, that's all right then," I said, smearing just a tad of six on the tip of my nose and subsiding. But then I started thinking.

"Marlene? What's the etiquette on tits? I mean, there yours are, where all the guys in the house could look at them if they weren't so intent on playing Boggle. You've obviously made a policy decision. How far does it go? If guests drop by, will you still bare them?"

"Yes," she said.

"And if we give a cocktail party, not that we will, but if we do, will your knockers still be in evidence?"

"No," she decided, "not at a cocktail party. Mammaries might be a bit intrusive among the vodka-gimlet set. One or two guests could probably cope, but blatant boobs could cause consternation at a full-blown jamboree."

"What about when the maid's here?"

"Don't be silly. The maid is a Jehovah's Witness. She'd short-sheet the beds and put strychnine in the barbecue sauce."

"Which is potent enough as it is. What about the pool man?"

"The pool man will be thrilled. I can't wait to show my headlights to the pool man."

I paddled around the deep end for a bit, lost in thought. "Marlene?" I finally asked, "should I show mine, too? Manifest my mammaries?"

"If you like," she said.

I have two questions. Is there a way of formalizing this etiquette? Can we get somewhere beyond this "poolman—yes, maid—no" criterion? Some simple rules that will fit all occasions?

Also, and this is important, can you fathom why none of the guys even once looked up from their Boggle game? I was watching them closely.

Cleo

Dear Cleo,

Quite a game, Boggle. No nuance, no subtlety, just straightforward blood lust to get more words down on paper than your fellow human, who seems to be scribbling faster than the brain can think; whereas all your small pea-mind can discern from the jumble of letters confronting you is *eat, ate,* and *tea.* "Stop writing!" you shout, but they never do.

When playing Boggle, one loses all desire and capacity to believe in the great majesty of nature. A spider may be crawling up one's ankle, a girl may suddenly tear off the top of her bathing suit, but you don't care, since you've just found *steerage.*

But breasts. Marlene is wrong and a hussy. One must never bare them before someone who works for one. It isn't seemly; it could create confusion. Think of the poor pool man. "Is this broad coming on to me, or what?" he will rightly think. And then what?

One must also consider the attractiveness factor. We would think a fulsome sensuality like yours would look more alluring gathered cunningly and only partially spilling from a bikini top instead of flapping about in the breeze.

A crucial point: It may be problematical to let them loose around someone to whom you are wildly attracted, since your melons may express your feelings too explicitly and sooner than you may wish.

Social Arbiters

■

Dear Social Arbiters:

It's about my mate, whom I would like to call Gloria. She is a nightmare.

Not always, mind you. There have been times when I've called her my little dreamboat, and meant it.

But take my dearest Gloria to a restaurant and she turns ugly. You know how sometimes when you're sitting in a restaurant and it's freezing outside, but there's this bozo who insists on keeping the door wide open while he yells to someone on the street, or tries to find his wallet? Nine times out of ten, this bozo is Gloria. I have known her to put on lipstick while standing thusly.

After a disdainful sniff, she always sends back the wine. Sometimes four times. Her food, too; her meal is inevitably inedible.

Her tone with waiters never varies. She is a plantation owner dealing with a dim-witted slave. I realize there are times when waiters more than deserve this, but some of them are perfectly pleasant human beings, with children and mates to feed.

Here's the worst: She kisses maitre d's. Calls them by their first names, has been known to punch them playfully on the arm. It's revolting to one who thinks of maitre d's as nothing more than primeval ooze.

Do not think that I am such a wimp that I take this lying down. We have had many a knockdown, drag-out battle over these restaurant antics. She promises to change. So far, this change has been imperceptible.

Malcolm

Dear Malcolm:

One can only feel sad for you. You have saddled yourself with a thoughtless person.

It would be simple if your Gloria only lacked empathy; empathy grows and flourishes as one gets older. But instead she seems to lack an alarmingly important attribute: critical distance.

Without the ability to step back and see how her behavior influences the greater flow of humanity, this poor sap is marooned on an island of self-involvement and stupidity. She simply does not understand why people get irritated; it isn't part of her mental repertoire.

Your poor Gloria is a cripple. If you want her to behave, you'll have to bribe her. Tell her if she's pleasant to everyone in restaurants for a month, you'll buy her a nice sweater.

Social Arbiters

■

Dear Social Arbiters:

Did you ever spend $26 on a ham with which to entice a prospective sweetheart? And did you ever invite one of your so-called buddies to join you in this $26 ham plus plenty of trimmings, along with the male of her choice?

And did this alleged buddy then not only arrive one male-of-her-choice short, but actually make a major play for your prospectives?

I mean, did she kind of rub her tit into his shoulder when she brought him the ham to be sliced, then press her knee against his while passing the potatoes, and then be so eager to show him her cleavage that she came a hair's breadth from dipping those aforementioned tits in the gravy? And when you went into the kitchen to get the apple crumble, did she kiss him flat on the mouth and ask him for a date?

Did this sort of thing ever happen to you? Well, me neither.

But it did happen to a very close, very dear friend of mine, and she wants to know what to do. She's frantic. She's really angry. She would really like to break her other friend's face. What should she do?

Betrayed

P.S. Okay, you win, it's really me.

Dear You:

No, this has not happened to us, and it never will, because we would never under any circumstances buy a $26 ham.

We hate ham. It's salty and rubbery at the same time. It often becomes involved with glutinous jelly. People put raisin sauce on it, which is silly, or adorn it with pineapple rings, which is plain discouraging. Then there are the candied yams oft found in close proximity to ham, usually sporting tiny marshmallows. People eat them. The only kind of ham we like is fresh ham, which isn't ham at all.

But we digress.

The other problem with this meal of yours is that it's just too damned hospitable. Potatoes, gravy, and apple crumble all seem to shout "Y'all come back, hear?"

Possibly if your menu were more daunting, like medallions of brain *en croûte* with truffle and grapefruit compote, your alleged friend wouldn't have felt so cozy and ready to make new friends. Do you think it's possible that she just got carried away by the calories?

No, neither do I. There is no excuse for stealing another woman's boyfriend, potential or otherwise. The woman is clearly pond scum.

A little flirting is fine, *little* being the operative word. But breast-flaunting? Kissing on the mouth? Not on your bippy. This is a hard and fast rule of girlfriendhood. No woman needs friends she can't trust.

"But what about the man?" I hear many readers screaming. "Isn't he the one really to blame?"

Well yes, of course, that's a given. A man who starts stuff at such an early date is not even to be considered. He is merely dismissed.

But a girlfriend who betrays you is a much more serious issue. Because it's never simply about sex but instead belies a creepy, underhanded competitiveness. A woman who tries to steal your man will try to steal your job, will tell you that your green dress is enchanting when in fact you look bilious, will encourage you to eat three hot-fudge sundaes in a row.

Have her for breakfast.

Social Arbiters

■

Dear Social Arbiters:

I am a compulsive present buyer. The other day I had $150 with which to buy myself some nice summer clothes and I ended up buying things for my sister's baby and my piano teacher. Not a thing for yours truly.

Why am I like this? Do I have a deep-seated self-hatred? How can I get rid of it?

Rose

Dear Rose:

Everyone in the world has a deep-seated self-hatred, except possibly Grace Jones.

You're simply generous, a rare and exotic trait in the 1980s, and you'd better not tell anyone or they'll try and study you under microscopes and the *National Enquirer* will be camping in your bushes.

Social Arbiters

■

Dear Social Arbiters:
I hear that you can tell what kind of lover a man is by the way he dances. Is this true?
Melissa

Dear Melissa:
Yes, it's simple. A man who is a good dancer is not a good lover. No one knows why this is true. No evidence about women has yet been published.
Social Arbiters
■

Dear Social Arbiters:
What happens when you are very, very sad, miserable, and foul-tempered for a very real and specific reason and you've got a best friend who is pirouetting on cloud nine for precisely the opposite reasons?

My heart is broken. I want to crawl under a rock and die. Almost. Oh sure, I know I'll get better, thank you, but right now the last thing I need is my pal smiling and grinning and looking all misty and cute because she just met the fellow of her dreams and she's got all her bags packed to go to Europe with him and she even showed me the excruciatingly sweet lacy white underwear she plans to wear on the plane.

I'm sitting here writing this just to keep my mind off my problems, which is hard to do with her in the room since at fifteen-minute intervals she throws her hands in the air and yells, "I'm so excited!"

"Bah! Humbug!" doesn't even begin to encompass my feelings. I know I should be happy for her, but it's so hard not to throttle her.
Distraught

Dear Distraught:

If she has a new man, that means that moments ago she didn't have anybody, and probably at some interval before that she broke up with someone else and was sad.

And if your heart is broken, there obviously was a time not too long ago when your heart wasn't broken, probably (in the great tradition of cosmic jokes) just when your friend's was. She probably came to you, tears streaming down her face, white and shaken and panicked, and you probably sang a little tune and said, "What do I care? I'm in love with the most wonderful man in the world!"

There is little worse than a friend who hates you when you're happy. Such behavior is undermining and possibly even psychologically dangerous. Swallow your grief for the moment. Feign jollity. As soon as her plane is in the air, you may resume the racking sobs.

Social Arbiters

■

Dear Social Arbiters:

I got married recently and already my husband seems to be looking up other women's dresses. In fact, at our actual wedding party, he lay flat on the floor just so he could see up my friend's dress. What should I do? Yell at him? Cry? Pretend I find this amusing?

Mary

Dear Mary:

The minute a man gets married, he starts looking up other women's dresses. It's inevitable. Pay no attention.

Social Arbiters

■

Dear Social Arbiters:

I've got this friend who could easily impersonate a beanpole. This girl can't go into a strong wind without stuffing her coat pockets with iron filings. Often when we're in a crowded room I can't find her at all. The words skinny, waiflike, and emaciated don't begin to do her justice.

Guess what? She's on a diet. I know, I can't believe it either. But yesterday I went to her office when she was just beginning her lunch—two baby tins of tomato juice, one tiny container of low-fat cottage cheese, and a little plastic bag of assorted greenery that she very carefully spread over the cottage cheese. I thought I would die. Then (you won't believe this either) she carefully scrutinized the side of each container for caloric content and entered her findings into a little book!

"It's really groovy how they tell you the calories of everything now," she told me.

"This is some kind of weirdo, perverto, sicko joke," I said. "Why, you have hardly any body at all."

"But I've gained three pounds," my friend said pertly. "You have to nip these things in the bud."

Bud? What bud is this? Nip it where? If there's any bud nipping to be done, it should be by me. I'm your average girl—not fat, but it would please me, and everyone who has to look at me, if I were to lose ten pounds. So when I see this woman, who resembles nothing so much as a fat string, eating rabbit food, I go mental. Even on the best occasions she makes me feel like a baby elephant. Now I feel like two baby elephants. How can I stop this human strand?

Jessica

Dear Jessica:

Here's the bitter truth: Even a criminally thin woman can get hysterical about her body.

Your friend probably nonchalantly stepped on the scale one morning, thinking of nothing in particular until her eye fell upon the gauge. Then, I can guarantee you, her teensy stomach dropped into her ankles and her brain flew through the top of her head. She became so weak she collapsed onto her bed in a fever of agitation, muttering, "Oh my God oh my God this is the beginning of the end! Today three pounds, tomorrow Lane Bryant!"

Another, happier truth: we all picture ourselves approximately fifteen pounds heavier than we actually are. You, in fact, are obviously five pounds underweight, so forget the elephant motif, forget your pal's mania, and have a nice chocolate bar.

Social Arbiters

■

Dear Social Arbiters:

I have present-giving anxiety. I'm sitting here wrapping Christmas presents for all my friends and becoming increasingly convinced that Emily will hate the black satin bed jacket, Maggie will simply despise the pigskin address book, Lynn will look at the cashmere teddy in disbelief, and Annabel will smile saccharinelike at the hand-rolled chocolates.

Last Christmas I got so crazy I pretended I didn't have time to buy anybody anything and shoved the already-wrapped presents under the bed. They're still there.

I don't know, I just start feeling horribly presumptuous, foisting my taste on others. Am I a loony?

Brenda

Dear Brenda:

We love a sensitive person.

But sensitivity can so easily turn into an albatross. Get those presents out from under your bed immediately; you will now have room for all those old sweaters you can't bear to part with.

For the future, we shall give you a valuable gift-giving tip: When shopping, pretend you're a method actor who is about to open in the role of the gift-givee. Let's call him Jonathan.

When you go into a shop, make sure you *are* Jonathan—imagine yourself with his nose, his eyes, his slight paunch, his hysterical fear of shag rugs. Peruse the pima cotton shirts and argyle socks with Jonathan-eyes. When your glance suddenly lights on a pair of silly leather suspenders, you will *be* Jonathan and you will know that you love them.

Meanwhile, keep wrapping with equanimity. There is not one woman (or many men, either) in existence who would pass up the presents you describe. In fact, they constitute our Christmas list.

Social Arbiters

SELF-HELP

COMPLAINING: A PASSÉ PASTIME

I don't want to hear about it.

I don't want to hear about anything. I've had it. I'm throwing in the towel before I drown in complaints.

This is my new rule: Everyone must practice sunniness.

Say your girlfriend's left you because you're too fat. Your immediate response will be to call me, since on every bathroom wall in the city are penciled the words. "For a good moan, call Cynthia 555-1212."

Take your finger from that dial, unless you are prepared to have the following conversation:

You· Hello, Cynthia?

Me· Yes, what is it?

You· I've just called to tell you how wonderful you are.

Me· What else?

You· I saw some dresses you'd really like in this great shop the other day. Very nice designs. Perfect for you.

Me· You interest me strangely. Tell me more.

You· I will, but why don't we have lunch tomorrow? There's a new French restaurant right in your neighborhood. *Trés* good. Since I've just gotten a big residual check, it's on me.

Me· I've never fully realized what a wonderful human being you are. Anything else new?

You· Not really, except I may have to cut down on the profiteroles with chocolate sauce.

Me· What do you mean?

You· Oh nothing, it's too tedious to go into right now. I'll see you tomorrow. Good-bye.

I believe the whole trend started on Nov. 23, 1963, when those of us who were alive were traumatized. The President! Shot! What could it mean? We all became sad, disillusioned, weird. We knew nothing was what it seemed, so we created the sixties, where nothing even pretended to be what it seemed but that made it really fun. Then all our toys were taken away and it was the seventies.

When things got ugly. When gut-spilling was the name of the game. When half the population was sticking fingers down their throats and retching as part of their morning ritual, the other half was primally screaming, and everyone would discuss it at length over dinner (miso soup and brown rice cutlets). Then there were those piquant open marriages, est, immersion tanks, rolfing, transcendental meditation, transactional analysis, and people wearing orange for religious reasons.

We were so zealous! Every naked, greedy little need was exposed, dissected, cataloged. Every personality trait was traced, each sexual thrust discussed.

Some of us still spend our lives figuring out how to live them, but most of us don't do this anymore. The sixties (disillusionment, euphoria, disillusionment), the seventies (self-absorption), and the eighties (fabulousness) have swum together in our heads and made us cynical. We know everything now, and it all sucks.

The world is coming to an end (amen), all men be slime (hallelujah), and nothing will ever work out (praise the lord!).

Where does this leave us? Complaining. Complacently masochistic. We have developed a vast vocabulary of selfdom, on which we have now superimposed this new cynicism. We had better all join hands and walk into the sea, or shut up.

Here are the things I never want to hear about:

• How your lover was really a bastard last night when you woke him up at 5 A.M. to ask him what he meant when he said, "I have a stomachache."

• Why your boss is a filthy pig and doesn't understand you or appreciate you and anyway you're not making enough money and why should you, an artist, have to compromise, have to sell your soul for the almighty dollar, which hardly goes anywhere these days, since at your last trip to the supermarket you spent $45.72 on some fresh-squeezed orange juice and the tiniest tin of pesto imaginable.

• Why there's no point in going to the movies anymore, or reading magazines, or seeing a play, or watching television, because it all sucks, sucks, sucks. Intellectual life in America is on an irretrievable decline and you have decided, as a protest, to commit suicide.

• How you met this actor the other night at the Palladium and he was drunk and a bunch of people came back to your place including the actor but you didn't get his phone number, or his last name. But the thing is, you're in love with him, no, honestly, you are. And if I'm really a friend to you, I'll figure out how to find him and then how to get him to make a commitment.

• How you've just decided that your therapist is misguided and neurotic and secretly hostile toward you.

• How no one in the world loves you, or could ever love you the way you are.

Now it is true that we all have troubles, heartbreaks, tragedies. But I hate to see us all becoming so *proud* of them. Yes, life is mainly dreadful, but whining is passé. Let's be plucky, let's be staunch. We can always make jokes or start a revolution, whichever seems more practical.

Or, when things get really beyond the pale, we can pretend we're in a sit-com.

THE SITCOM WAY OF BEING

All happy families live a situation comedy, all unhappy families live a soap opera. This is the sad truth. The happy truth is that you get to choose. Take my life (please):

• *We're moving.* The financial permutations and complications have transcended terrifying and are now bloodcurdling. Plus there are minor annoyances like the telephone company charging $200 to install service. We have no furniture, yet I spend all my time looking at wallpaper samples until I get dizzy and have to put my head between my legs.
• *The kid is auditioning for the vocal department of Music and Art High.* He needs a song to sing, he doesn't know what. His lips curl in contempt at well-meant adult suggestions like "Blowin' in the Wind" and "Begin the Beguine."
• *There's somebody I'm seeing.* At least I think I am. We take walks to the butcher, go to the odd party. Is it too soon? Am I misreading everything? Plus I took a little trip recently where I struck up an innocent flirtation with a very cute guy, a printer. I guess he was only kidding, but he asked me to marry him.
• *Lucy's mother died.* Lucy called at 2 A.M. the other

morning, sobbing hysterically about getting the next plane to England. We stayed up all night staving off the heebie-jeebies, spent the next day getting traveler's checks, a black veil, black stockings, dinner, and an emergency shrink appointment.

• *My oldest and dearest friend called to say that after seven years, his lover no longer loved him.* He was wondering if he'd be able to sleep.

• *The funniest writer I know took me to dinner to tell me he probably would never write again.* What will I read?

• *My mother says she can either afford groceries or repairs to her car, not both.* Also why haven't I been to visit her?

• *In precisely two days I have to stand up in front of an audience and speak for an hour.* I have not figured out what to say.

• *After I move, I must go to England.* But I haven't figured out who's staying with the kid.

• *Injudicious pictures of me in a bubble bath have been circulated.*

• *The kitchen ceiling is falling in.* Every ten minutes a piece of plaster the size of a dinner plate falls onto the stove.

What does one do with a life like this? The obvious answer, at least for a girl with a Jewish upbringing, is to go all soap opera. Wringing hands, flooding tears, endless cups of coffee in depressingly clean kitchens. Swells of violin music after each fight and each traumatic encounter. Sudden drinking bouts. Dumb dialogue. It's so easy to slip straight into the sticky morass of the soap. But instead, after years of rigorous anxiety, I have found the true road to personal fulfillment.

It's simple. I pretend I'm in a sitcom.

I'll tell you my secret method, which you can practice in your own home for fun and profit.

1 LISTEN TO THE LAUGH TRACK IN YOUR MIND Just beneath the surface of consciousness, there lurks in every human a subterranean giggle. Encourage this giggle. Nurture it, give it its space, and it will be fruitful and multiply and cheer your days and warm your nights. This subterranean giggle is the wellspring of all human goodness. It is always at the ready to get us through our hairiest moments.

Everybody gets pregnant at once?

The report card blows out the window?

The entire football team of Cambridge University is sleeping on your living room floor?

Mercury is retrograde?

Picture yourself in the above situations (all of which have happened to me!). Horrible, or funny? If you're not sure, pretend everything is accompanied by a cameraman and a laugh track. It's all funny if you let it be. Even death, the biggest joker of them all.

2 DIVIDE YOUR LIFE INTO HALF-HOUR SEGMENTS, allowing for commercial breaks.

For example:

It's 2:30 P.M. and my mother calls to say she's feeling faint but hasn't any money for food, but don't worry, she'll be fine. Then the doorbell rings and it's the cute printer who's been up all night driving to my door. He wants to consummate our relationship. "Gotta go, mom," I say and hang up the phone, which rings again. It's the travel agent saying I must come and pick up the tickets right away. The printer is sitting on the couch singing "Yesterday" with my son as a crash is heard from the kitchen and the doorbell rings at the same time. At the door are both a contractor and the man I think I may be seeing, who both come in. Another chunk of the ceiling falls on the contractor's head while the man I think I'm seeing engages in stilted conversation with the printer and the kid sings "Yesterday" louder and louder. Then my friend who is heartbroken drops by with the writer who has decided not to write and everybody decides it would be nice if I made a cup of tea.

Funny, or what?

Then it's time for the commercial break, when I pretend to be out of milk and go out of the male-infested apartment. I sit on the stoop for ten minutes watching a dog decide whether she's going to pee or not until the second segment, when I go back into the house to find the printer engaged in a long-distance conversation with Lucy, who's calling to tell me about the funeral. "Shut up!" I say to the kid who is now twanging an electric guitar. The kid says he's tired of life, is running away from home, puts his coat on. "Where's the milk?" calls my heartbroken friend from the kitchen, where he is communing with the contractor, who is holding an ice pack to his head. "Maybe if we could collaborate on something, I could write again," says the retired writer. "I can see I'm not wanted here," says the man I think I am seeing. "Wait up, kid." As they leave, my editor calls and wants to know about those pictures in the bubble bath. Then the phone company calls and says they need another $200. "Do you want this tea or what?" says the heartbroken man, who stalks out when I say no. "I'm going too," says the writer who can't write. "It's clear you're not interested." "It's impossible to fix without taking the ceiling down," says the contractor as he tracks plaster dust everywhere. "I'll send you an estimate next week."

"Alone at last," says the printer.

CURTAIN

See how easy?

Don't forget to take copious notes and look at your life from many different camera angles. Try to remember that you don't want many outdoor scenes; they're too expensive. Then write everything down in script form and you will have in your possession a pilot, plus several episodes, and you only must turn them in to the network of your choice to become a millionaire.

WHAT DRUGS WILL DO TO YOU IF YOU LET THEM

I ▪ ECSTATIC—TRAUMATIC

Perhaps you're like me and never get around to things. Oh, we mean to, when we hear about these things that are simply the latest and greatest and will without question revolutionize humanity as we know it.

But usually when we're finding out about the one thing that will revolutionize humanity as we know it it's about four in the morning and we're somewhat blotto and not paying attention.

Of course we're sorry later, when everybody in the world already knows about this new thing that will revolutionize humanity as we know it except us, and we're afraid to ask for details. The ship has passed us by. Sometimes it has passed us by so far that the thing that will revolutionize humanity as we know it has been outlawed, and possession of same will ensure a stiff prison sentence. This is always a hell of a note.

So maybe at this late date—who knows?—you may be about ready to try that revolutionary drug called ecstasy. If so, here's a possible scenario, totally and completely made up and nothing but a product of my imagination:

There you are, hanging around somewhere raw and strange like a new after-hours club, waiting for someone whose boyfriend knows someone whose girlfriend just got back from England with a suitcase full of illicit ecstasy. ("Oh why," you ask yourself, smiting your forehead, "why do I have to be such a lazy, procrastinating goop? Why can't I decide to do a drug *before* it becomes a felony?")

The ecstasy dealer materializes somewhere around 5 A.M. Someone catches sight of her brocade-clad figure snaking through the throngs of revelers, someone else follows her into the bathroom, a sudden flurry of money-exchanging takes place, and suddenly there you are clutching this tiny brown capsule. A small headache appears above your left eye as you realize you're stricken with terror.

"You sure I won't go mental?" you ask the friend who's next to you, washing down his capsule with a swig of vodka-and-grapefruit. "You're sure I won't go stark-staring mad and tear off my clothes and start seeing God and dance on tables and break out into a 'cold sweat and scream and scream?"

"It's nothing like that," the friend says, emitting a reassuring chuckle. "You'll just feel good and you'll love everybody in the whole world and you'll have fun, fun, fun."

"Do you feel anything yet?" you ask after fifteen minutes.

"Almost," he says. "I think maybe. Sort of."

"How about now?" you ask after half an hour.

"I'm definitely beginning to feel it," he states. "Doesn't your scalp feel all kind of tingly?"

"Tingly how?"

"Well, like the hairs might be doing a little dance on it. And what about your sound perception? Is there maybe a sort of almost imperceptible echo? Kind of?"

"Oh sure, I think," you say. "Just a faint echo. I thought it was a headache, but now I see I was wrong. And you know, it's slightly possible that I might be feeling just the teensiest bit dizzy."

"God, I'm really feeling *great!*" your friend shrieks maybe twenty minutes later, as he stands up and twirls around in faster and faster circles. "Whee!" he continues. "Don't you feel wonderful?"

"Probably," you say. "I think I'll go to the bathroom."

Waiting for the toilet, you meet a filmmaker. "There's

nothing I like better than doing cocaine and drinking white wine and then doing a joint to top it off," the filmmaker says. A wave of nausea almost knocks you over.

With a certain difficulty you find your way back to your friend, who now has three girls with large breasts and tiny waists attached to him as he whirls in his circles.

"Just a little bit sick to my stomach, a small headache," you say. "I think it's time to go home."

"Where are the stairs?" you think. "Will I fall down? Do I have cigarettes? Where do I live? Did I have a coat?" Your head is now pealing.

Down the stairs. Twenty more. Five more, doin' just great. Cabs, hundreds of them. Which one for you? Oh, please, a driver who won't talk, or smell, or want a date.

In the cab, momentary money-panic, then key-panic.

You walk up four flights to your door, head throbbing, feet stumbling, throw the keys down, sink onto the bed.

"I must get up," you tell yourself. "I must take off my clothes and put my nightgown on. That's it, that's the girl. Now the sweater, very nice, now the stockings. Fold them up carefully, show who's in control. Hang the skirt up, excellent." Nightgown on, you crawl under the covers, turn out the light, and close your eyes.

Then you open your eyes, turn the light back on, push the covers down, lurch to your feet, walk carefully to the bathroom, find the toilet, and violently vomit.

"Oh dear, oh dear," you say to yourself. "Missed. Goodness me. Well, that'll be okay. Just clean it up. Oh dear, on the nightgown, too. Just take the nightgown off, run it under cold water. No, hot water. But what about the rest? How about paper towels? In the kitchen!"

And suddenly an intense Annie Hall fantasy occurs: Call up the ex-boyfriend, very Diane Keaton. "It's me, please come over. I've just puked all over the bathroom, ha ha. I don't know. I just missed. I miss you. Please come over, help me clean it up. Then put me to bed, tuck me in. A small kiss on the brow, maybe a nice soothing fondle."

But will he liken a pool of puke to a Buick? And he's the Diane Keaton character in this relationship, not you! Get the paper towels, you wimp! You sniveler! And some Fantastik, goddamnit! Can't have germs!

The nice cop–mean cop arguing in your head gets you through it, helps to find another nightgown and get you back under the covers, where you lie and wonder about all the warm and wonderful psychological revelations you're supposed to be having for your twenty dollars.

"I'm too full of self-pity, that's it," you say to yourself as full daylight breaks through the curtains and you fall asleep.

II ■ WHY COCAINE IS BAD FOR YOU

A COCAINE TURNS YOU INTO A MORON   This is the scariest part. Turning into a moron is the biggest threat that faces humankind today. One day you may be a sensible member of the species, the next you are a whimpering lumpish substance with a bit of spittle oozing from the corner of your mouth. Scientists are baffled by this burgeoning phenomenon! They think it may be related to the dumping of toxic wastes. But it isn't. It's cocaine.

You take it. You like it. You take a little more. You like it even better. "Good stuff, this," you think. "I guess I'll just do it all the time." And then you'll think, "Sure, I used to be a brilliant flute player (or art director, or filmmaker, or mathematical theoretician, or race car driver) but I don't care about that now. I think I'll just freebase once, what the hell."

Before you know where you are, you will have eschewed your lovely career and tried to become a cocaine dealer, with pitiful results. "Only for a little while," you tell yourself.

And the next thing you know it's twenty years later and you're cleaning windshields on the Bowery. For a quarter.

B COCAINE TURNS YOU INTO A MORON There you'll be, at a perfectly darling birthday party, having a nice chat with the birthday boy, who happens to be English, straight, and cute. Just your type, in fact. Just as you've got a good flirtation flourishing, some guy with a little vial approacheth. "Want some?" he asks innocently.

"Sure," you say, you fool.

Next thing you know, you and the cute English guy are talking fifteen to the dozen and not listening even slightly to what the other says, since both of you have your eyes glued to the man with the vial, hoping he'll come back.

And come back he will, and he'll invite you to another party. Visions of more cocaine will dance in your greedy head, and you'll go with him.

At 6 A.M. you will become aware you are perched on the arm of a frayed armchair in a seedy apartment on East Third Street, surrounded by overflowing ashtrays and empty beer bottles with twelve strangers who are grinning insanely at each other and cleaning their nasal passages with water.

None of these twelve strangers, you'll realize, has a brain bigger than a pea. And neither do you. The cute English guy has disappeared; you've forgotten all about him anyway.

C COCAINE TURNS YOU INTO A MORON Somehow you're in a nightclub ladies' room. The water from one of the overflowing toilets is congealing around your ankles, but you don't care, you're stuffing your nose.

Then you must have a drink. Jack Daniel's, double, down the hatch.

Some acquaintances approach. Kiss kiss. How are you? Oh, just fabulous, how are you?

"You know what I just love about you?" you'll find yourself saying ten minutes later, and this to a man who you once knew five years ago when you were both working for a sleazy ad agency and looking for your big break in the conceptual art field. "I just love your mind. Your mind is just so great. You think about things. You're not just another asshole on the club scene. You know?"

"God, I know," he'll say, putting a chummy arm around your shoulder. "And I'll tell you why. It's because I live in New Jersey. I *need* my solitude to become myself, the person I am—sensitive and warm and deeply, intensely caring. I just float around in my swimming pool, meditating on life, wondering how I, just one man, can contribute to humanity. Like another hit? Here you go. Now the other one. Okay? Anyway, you gotta come out to the house. I'll tell you what! Come for the weekend! All right? It'll be great. Bring your bathing suit! Bring all your friends!"

"Who the hell was that guy?" you'll wonder to the friend you dragged to the club the night before.

"How should I know?" your friend will say. "I heard he ran brothels. But the way you were acting, I figured he was your long-lost lover."

"Are you crazy? I don't even like him."

"Funny, then, how you told him all about every relationship you ever had and how he's different and how you'll be happy to move in with him and have his children."

"Oh my God," you'll say.

FEAR OF DATING

The realization hit me heavily, like a .44 Magnum smashing into my skull. My heart started beating with a quick dread, and my blood froze in my veins. My stomach did backflips; I had to race to the bathroom to avoid a major incident. The ordeal I was about to face is one of the most grisly, macabre, and chilling experiences known to woman.

Dating. I will have to start dating again.

Please God no, don't make me do it! I'll be good from now on, I promise! I'll stop feeding the dog hashish! I'll wear that mauve acrylic sweater my grandmother knitted me! I'll never again have ten pizzas with extra cheese delivered to the Kiwi! I'll be kind, thoughtful, sober, industrious—anything. But please God, not the ultimate torture of dating!

I mean, I can't even stand the thought of the shower beforehand, and the shower used to be my favorite ritual, giving my hair three sudsings for good measure, thoughtfully shaving my legs way past my knees, keeping my face under the hot stream of water until every old crust of mascara was dissolved.

That's why I stayed with him so long, probably. I couldn't stand going through it all again. Sure, he might be a trifle wild and intractable, I kept telling myself, but at least I know I'll get laid tonight, and tomorrow night. At least he'll be used to the fact that I try on seven outfits so that I'll look okay when I run to the corner for a quart of milk. At least someone will go to the movies with me and not try to hold my hand.

Hand-holding—the worst thing about dating. The fellow, or maybe even I, will decide that holding hands is a sweet simple way to start. Hah! It's the most nerve-racking experience of life! Once I start holding hands, I'm afraid to stop. If I pull my hand away, will he think I'm being cold, or moody? Should I squeeze his hand and kind of wiggle my fingers around suggestively? Or is that too forward? What if we're holding hands in the movies and I have to scratch my nose? If I let his hand go, and then scratch the offending nose, and then don't grab his hand again immediately, will he think I'm rejecting him? Will he be relieved? What if my hand is clammy? A clammy hand is more offensive than bad breath or right-wing politics! A clammy hand means you are a lousy lay! Everybody knows that!

And what, dear spiteful God, will I wear? I'll need new dresses, new jewelry, new sweaters, trousers, underwear. And shoes! Shoes tell everything; shoes have to be perfect! Men like high heels, right? I can't walk in high heels. Well, I can try. For a really important date, I can just see myself spending $250 on a pair of drop-dead suede heels, maybe with some fanciful stitching and sweet bows to tie around my ankles. This time it will be different, I'll tell myself; this time I will be able to walk. But after an hour the ball of my foot will cramp up, I know it, and I'll hobble. "Is anything wrong?" he'll ask me solicitously. "You're limping." And I won't know where to look. I won't be able to say, "These fucking shoes are crippling me and if I don't take them off this minute I'll be maimed for life," because then he'll know I just bought them, that I bought them to go out on a date with him. And that will make him feel weird and pressured knowing that this date was a big deal for me and he'll realize that maybe I'm not as popular and sophisticated as he thought I was if I had to buy a special pair of shoes that I can't even walk in for chrissakes just for a date with *him*. So I have to explain the limping in such a way that it won't have to do with the shoes. An old war wound? Fell down the stairs earlier?

What if my hair refuses to behave? What if it's all recalcitrant and cranky and goes all limp and flat on one side and then sort of bends at a right angle over one ear? I mean, sometimes I apply precisely the right amount of mousse and hang upside down when I blow-dry it and yet something still goes drastically wrong and I end up looking like Margaret Thatcher. Sometimes the suspense of what I will look like is so terrible that I have to take a Valium.

I have been known to apply four shades of lipstick, one on top of the other, in a pathetic attempt to achieve a certain I'm-not-actually-wearing-lipstick-I-just-naturally-have-pink-moist-luscious-lips effect. I have been known to put green eye pencil below my lower lashes, look in the mirror, realize that I look like a gangrenous raccoon, quickly remove it, look in the mirror, realize that I'd rather look like a gangrenous raccoon than an anemic buffalo, and reapply the stuff. I have been known to start trying on outfits in an entirely tidy room and somehow when I am finished every single item of clothing I own is off the rack and on the floor and then when the phone rings there is no way on earth I can find it. I can't even find my *bed*. God, I hate dating.

And when he rings my doorbell and my stockings are still around my ankles because my garter belt is missing but with mad, deep, quick thought I finally remember it's in my black satin purse (don't ask) and I get it on and get the stockings up and answer the door smiling casually, what precisely do I say?

What will I talk about on a date?

Not one thing that's on my mind will be a suitable topic of conversation. "Do you think we'll sleep together tonight?" "Are you one of those guys who can't make a commitment? Or can only make a commitment to a woman with really smooth, finely muscled thighs?" "Is my deodorant working?" "What kind of relationship did you have with your mother?" "How do you think we're getting along so far?" "Do you like me?" "How much do you like me?" "Are you sure you really like me?" "Have you happened to contract any exotic social diseases?" "Ever been plagued by impotence?" "You're not going out with me because you feel sorry for me, are you?"

No, we'll talk about movies. What we've seen recently. What if he tells me that he finally got around to seeing *Cocoon* and it turned out to be one of the greatest experiences of his life? Will I pretend to agree? I bet I will. I bet something slimy inside myself will cause me to nod my head encouragingly and say, "Yes, wasn't it lovely? I especially liked the sex scene in the pool." And then I'll hate myself because I've turned our date into a tissue of lies. I'll become distracted thinking about what a hypocrite I really am and my eyes will glaze over and I'll nod absently when he tries to draw me out and then he'll get all paranoid, thinking I hate him because he liked *Cocoon*. He'll be right.

But what if it turns out that his favorite movie is *The Man Who Came to Dinner*, with *Slapshot* a close second? Then I could fall in love. Then I'll really be terrified.

WHEN IN DOUBT, ACT LIKE MYRNA LOY

Just for a gag, take this quiz:

1 There you are, being pulled along the floor of an incredibly posh drinking establishment by a small, strongly effusive fox terrier. The dozens of wrapped Christmas presents that were once in your arms are now scattered in every direction. You finally

BUT ENOUGH ABOUT YOU

come to rest, and happen to glance up. Your husband, dressed impeccably and holding a martini, is looking down at you, astonished. At this point, do you
A Burst into tears and demand to be taken home?
B Grasp your husband around his ankles, pleading forgiveness and promising never to do it again?
C Simulate an epileptic fit?
D Pick yourself up, brush yourself off, and say, "Oh, so it's you! He's dragged me to every gin mill on the block."

One more, for luck:

2 Your husband is about to go off on a dangerous adventure. To make sure he doesn't leave you behind, you get into the taxi before him. Your husband tells the cabbie to take you to Grant's tomb and the taxi speeds away with only you inside. When your husband enquires later how you liked Grant's tomb, you say
A You are a filthy pig and I want a divorce immediately.
B I'll never get over what you've done to me.
C Please may I have a sedative?
D It was lovely. I'm having a copy made for you.

If I know you, you smart cookie, you answered *D* to both the above questions. As well you should. It's exactly what Myrna Loy would have done. Did.

If you've ever seen *The Thin Man*, with Myrna Loy as Nora Charles, you recognize these scenes. But these are more than simply great moments in cinematic history; they are behavioral lessons on which one can base one's life. Forget est, forget years of grueling psychotherapy, forget taking off your clothes in the presence of other consenting adults and "sharing" your most excruciating childhood memories.

I sure have. Whenever I'm too crazy, too paranoiac, or too mentally feeble to deal with a situation, I pretend I'm Myrna Loy. It works.

Consider: the Myrna Loy who appeared as Nora in *The Thin Man* movies was a real pip. She was beautiful, she was witty, she was self-possessed, she was adventuresome, she wore great hats. (*Note*: If you're a man, it might be more profitable to pretend you're William Powell as Nicky, another perfect role model.)

When Nora discovered that Nicky had had six martinis to her paltry one, she told the barman to "bring me five more martinis, Bill, line 'em up right here." When Nicky took her to her first jazz club, she was bemused for a moment, but before he knew it she was saying to some creep, "Oh, get lost, you off-beat rinky-dink, you're nowhere!" When Nicky happened to ask her if she possessed a nice evening gown, she didn't blink or twiddle her fingers or pick her nose but said straightaway, "Yes, I've got a lulu. Why?"

This is all good stuff.

Movie stars have traditionally been used as role models; that's what they're there for. But so many of us pick silly ones to ape. Who can forget 1976, when every third woman in the world decided she was *exactly* like Diane Keaton in *Annie Hall*? Everywhere one went that year, one ran into hordes of females in baggy trousers and their boyfriend's ties, stuttering and saying "lah-di-dah, lah-di-dah." Most depressing. And who will ever get over that ghastly moment in history when otherwise sensible women decided to act just like Liza Minnelli in *Cabaret* and painted their fingernails green while discussing "divine decadence"? Soon after, one could not leave one's home without colliding with hordes of women wearing artfully and expensively ripped sweatshirts and the sultry, vapid look of some person called, I believe, Jennifer Beales.

Modern movie stars will get you nowhere, role model—wise. I can't think of one who has wit, moral integrity, and terrific outfits. One must stick with the old girls, who knew what was what.

Instead of Myrna Loy, you may if you wish emulate Lauren Bacall in *To Have and Have Not*, the one where she asks, "You know how to whistle, don't you?" Or Katharine Hepburn in *The Philadelphia Story*. Or Bette Davis in *All About Eve*.

But I personally stick with Myrna. She's got the lightest touch. Who else could play poker with the boys in the baggage car and never remove her hat? Who else, when Nicky was ogling a stacked heiress, could say, "The earrings are higher up?" and leave it at that?

I'm not kidding; I really do this. Not, mind you, as a matter of course, since I often have a perfectly fine personality of my own, and one must, whenever possible, to one's own self be true.

But there are times when I am completely boggled—I know for a fact that the minute I open my mouth, I'm going to turn into my mother, my grandmother, or my Aunt Selma. Which is unfortunate, since my family were all very big on a particularly noxious brand of sullen martyrdom.

Witness last summer. There I was, minding my own business, when the Kiwi suddenly turned horrible. He became furiously impatient with me because I was afraid to climb a (small) mountain in the dark and left me alone on some wet rocks while he went exploring. Even took my cigarette lighter.

When the thoughtless cad reappeared, my first impulse was to sniffle a lot. The first words that sprung to my mind went something like this:

"After all I've done for you, look how you treat me! [Sob.] You obviously don't care about me at all, oh no you don't, I can tell. [Stifled moans!] Oh, how could you? What have I done to deserve this?"

Awful. The worst thing about the what-have-I-done-to-deserve-this gag is that people will tell you. Had I said something along the lines of the above, Mr. Adorable would have felt perfectly justified in starting a huge row in which he touched upon all my inadequacies, fears, and lousy nutritional habits.

Luckily, some still voice of sanity cautioned me that this was the wrong tack, even though it was the one I was brought up with. And luckily, like a lightning bolt, Myrna Loy flashed through my sniveling brain. What would Myrna do in such a situation? Would one ever catch *her* being so wimpily wretched?

I held my piece during the car ride home, letting Loyness filter through my being. When we got inside the house, I calmly filled the kettle and put it on the stove. Then I turned around.

"Darling," I said, "you are an inconsiderate brat. I absolutely refuse to be left alone and terrified on any more dark mountainsides. Next time the climbing lust overtakes you, warn me first so that I can take in a nice, warm movie instead of sitting around like a fool on wet rocks, you abysmal warthog."

"But, but—" he said.

"Don't *but* me, you twit," I continued silkily. "I simply won't have it, and that's that."

All right, the words may have been a bit clumsy, since I had to write my own material on the spot. But things never got ugly. By morning he apologized prettily, I accepted him happily, and we were in perfect accord as I slipped into my satin dressing gown to go down to breakfast.

Myrna would have been proud.

MAKING FRIENDS WITH ANXIETY

Anxiety attack!

I'm on the subway and it's stopped I don't know why and I'm late already the car is packed and sharing the strap I'm hanging from is a little pale man with no eyelashes at all and he's—yes, *I'm not imagining it!*—he's rubbing his crotch against my thigh but I can't move away because I'm a sardine in here and I'm so late, will probably lose this job, is that a hand going into my bag? *I can't breathe.* Will the train move again? Never.

Anxiety attack!

It's ten-thirty at night I sent my son to the corner for milk at nine-thirty he's not back yet what's he doing, where is he, is he still alive? Although this is New York City I'll call the cops anyway. They won't come. They will come; they'll *laugh* at me getting hysterical. I'm waiting I'm waiting any second now he'll come through the door, "Mom!" and I'll break his jaw. *Where is he?* Decided to take a little stroll? Got into a car with a *child-molesting murderer?*

Anxiety attack!

Nothing is wrong. Everything's fine it's just that I wish I had a Valium because *my head hurts my heart's pounding I can't breathe.* I'm pacing. I'm frightened. My head is swimming with strange images. I'm running to the bathroom. I can't read, can't sleep, can't think. I'm going to die I can tell this is a death premonition. *Nothing's wrong! Really.*

Okay, I'm fine now.

If you've never had an anxiety attack, I don't want to know you. I'm sure you're very nice, very pleasant, but I can't relate. I once had a two-year anxiety attack (1973–75). Now I privately think of myself as a connoisseur of anxiety attacks, having successfully cataloged at least thirty-seven different variations of the species, each with its own piquant bouquet of emotions.

Here are some:

THE BLANCMANGE Hardly an anxiety attack at all, this is the normal state of consciousness for those of us in big cities. Unexpected sounds make the heart jump into the throat; a moving shadow glimpsed from the corner of the eye precedes a monster adrenaline rush. A huge crowd of business suits congesting the steps of a favorite and heretofore undiscovered eatery causes nausea and despondence.

THE PETITE WEIRDNESS There you are, minding your own business, when, suddenly and out of no-where, everything is *too much*. The man in front of you at the movie theater eating something wrapped in cellophane and telling his date what a fabulous *auteur* Sylvester Stallone is must be immediately assassinated. Your shopping bag disintegrates in the rain on Four-teenth Street and you must check into a mental hos-pital.

THE SUDDEN ABYSS These are the little pockets of dread that punctuate our days and riddle our nights. We're sitting happily at lunch and someone says some-thing like, "How's your book coming?" and we im-mediately need CPR. We're standing at the bar in the Mike Todd room and someone whispers, "Don't look now, but isn't that your ex-boyfriend over there?" and we consume three double tequilas before we know it.

THE FULL-THROTTLE BLOW-OUT The activity of the brain speeds up to 45 rpms while the rest of the body stays at 33⅓. This causes an insistent inner hum and a whirling sensation, which in turn produces a terrible and strange heart-throbbing and a desire for instant unconsciousness. Occasionally the mind ac-tually floats away from the body—the last thing you remember is being in a shop trying on a mauve sweater and how suddenly you're on a bus hurtling toward Cincinnati.

"Anger," your shrink will probably tell you while you quiver and shake with the heebie-jeebies. "Massive homicidal rage you felt against your parents as a child but which you considered inappropriate and dangerous since it would never do to do in mom and dad, so you took this blinding fury and turned it in upon yourself, where it has caused dreadful attacks which to this day cripple and inconvenience you."

"Pooh pooh," I say to shrinks, anxiety isn't that at all. Here's what anxiety *really* is:

Anxiety is your friend. Anxiety is telling you in the nicest possible way that you are being threatened and it really would be better for all concerned if you stopped lollygagging and did something, anything, instead of sitting around behaving helpless. Anxiety wants you to *do it now.*

Son missing? Go out and find him. Man rubbing against you against your will? Scream piercingly. Groceries all over the street? Pick them up. Ex-boyfriend sighted? Pour a drink over his head. Book not done? Get your agent to call your editor to say you've broken both arms.

"That's all very well," I hear you say, "but what about when I really *can't* do anything? What if my hands are tied? Like if it's my boss torturing me but I need the job or I'll starve. Or if it's Jerry Falwell?"

The solution is simple: Become a writer. Work hard and long until some publication somewhere gives you a column. Elbow your way into as much prominence as possible, and then write about people. By simply changing a name slightly, you can reduce to mincemeat any person, place, or thing that has incurred your displeasure. Remember: revenge is the best revenge.

IN THE ABYSS

I don't know whether to kill myself or go bowling.

—Florence Henderson
on "The Love Boat"

It looks all black outside, even at noon, and inside there is a perpetual dreary gray, wet and chill and noxious. I cannot clear my head of it; my eyes will hardly focus.

My arms and legs feel too heavy to move. If I could go into the kitchen to make coffee I would. There is no book to read, no one to speak to, nothing to occupy my hands, which won't move anyway.

The idea of love or hate or any strong passion is completely remote. I remember emotions as if from another life. Not all feeling has left, though: From my chest to my groin I feel a dull, constant ache, a pain it seems I have felt forever. I want to die.

I can't envision ever feeling whole, or vibrant, or jolly, or silly, or sweetly and innocently in love. I just look out the window, smoking cigarette after cigarette, the pain throbbing, the bed unmade.

"Will you look at this shameless slut? Three in the afternoon and she's lying there in her second-best nightgown," says Rita from the doorway.

"Pitiful," says Cleo, behind her.

"Honey, when was the last time you washed your hair?" Rita asks.

"How the hell did you get in here?" I say. "Go away, beat it. Piss off."

"I used my key," says Cleo. "You may have noticed

that you haven't been answering your phone—a sure attention-getter."

"Get up, get in that shower," says Rita.

I start to cry. Somebody cares.

"What's the matter with me?" I wail. "I think I'm having a nervous breakdown. I'm so frightened and confused and miserable. I lie around all day, being sucked deeper and deeper into some crazy black whirlpool of the soul. Then I try to go out, take a little walk in hopes that it will make me feel better. The minute I get outside my heart starts jumping into my throat and I panic. I think I am going to have a heart attack and die."

"You're heartbroken," says Cleo.

"You've been flirting too long with the abyss," says Rita. "You've fallen in. It's time to pull yourself out. Scramble up those rocks. Get dirt under your fingernails. Hang tough. Wait it out."

"Let's call Jake," says Cleo. "He can slap some sense into her."

"With friends like you, who needs a mother?" I ask. "And anyway, I'm not heartbroken."

"Nobody who wasn't heartbroken would let her hair get into such a state," says Rita.

Within my morass of misery, I can feel a few affectionate emotions stirring feebly. What girls. Cleo is picking the dead flowers out of a semi-live bouquet on my mantelpiece, wearing a little black miniskirt and big red sweater. Rita has gone into the kitchen and come back with a beer, which she drains in approximately five gulps, then daintily wipes her mouth. She is regarding me with slightly fearful consternation.

"There is a palpable haze of self-pity enveloping you. I can hardly see you. Take a shower. Wash your hair."

"Look," I say, "I am not heartbroken. I knew it would never work. He was too young, too cosmic. I loved him, though. We had some kind of fearsome, intense connection. We would look at each other and be hypnotized. The smell of him lost me to the rest of the world. I was disgusting. I would sniff his armpits like a greedy puppy sniffs a crotch. I remember the last time he sat on the edge of my bed, in an old pink T-shirt I bought him—the line of his torso was indescribably dear to me."

"Not heartbroken, hey?" says Cleo.

"Why not just pop into the shower and then tell us about it," says Rita, returning to her favorite motif. "I am not one of those people who gets her kicks from smelling pungent armpits."

I took an exploratory sniff. "Jesus, that proves it. I'm alive. Anyway, you don't understand. It's not about being heartbroken. I'm over that part. I'm sad, I'm resigned, I'm mending according to schedule. But this whole adventure has thrown me back on myself. I can't stand the sight of my inner self. It's all bleak and horrible and useless and aching and needy and lonely and desperate. I have no inner resources. Nothing will ever work."

"I have turned the shower water on," says Rita. "Get in there before I cut that nightgown off you with this pair of scissors I am brandishing."

"Fascist," I mutter.

I'm slicing half-inch hairs off my legs with a dreamy disposable when the door to the bathroom opens, the shower curtain is pushed aside.

"Jake, you pervert. Get out, I'm naked."

"I've seen them before, remember? Hi there, tits. Nice to see you again. Always loved them tits." He perches his big, burly self on the sink. "I'll just wait here until you're finished."

"I'm not going to kill myself in the shower, you know."

"Course not."

"I will be fine."

"Course you will. That boyfriend of yours is sleeping with someone else, I hear."

"He's not my boyfriend anymore."

"And you're not sleeping with anyone. The big old abandonment-goblin has got you in its clutches. You must feel like hell."

"This is not right, Jake. You were my boyfriend once too. Why are we talking about this?"

"This is where an old boyfriend can come in handy. I'm here to commiserate with you, fold you in my large and masculine embrace. Soothe your troubled brow. Feeling abandoned by a loved one is the worst pain there is."

"We had broken up. He has every right to go off with someone else."

"Course he does."

"Jake, I want to kill him. I want to take an ax and split his head open. I want to kick him so hard in the balls that he's doubled up for a month. I want to have him arrested."

"Come on out now, darling, you're getting water-logged."

Three hours later I am washed, dried, dressed, full of hamburger and three double tequilas, and I have just conked a man on the head with Jake's half-filled beer bottle.

"You are a half-witted, foul-faced, insane pervert!" I shriek to the guy I've attacked. Beer is streaming from his nose.

"This is good," says Rita, folding her arms and leaning back.

"She needed to get all that festering out of her system," says Cleo, watching the attacked guy beat a hasty retreat. "Mr. Cosmic has got himself another bimbo, she's gonna show him and everybody else by wasting away and letting her hair go all filthy. Silly cunt."

"I'm not heartbroken!" I scream at Jake as he tries to get me to sit on his lap. "I just simply don't want

to be alive anymore! Big fucking deal!" Then I pass
out.

"Things are not over between her and that Kiwi,"
says Cleo.

"Don't I know it," says Rita, signaling for the check.
"I can't wait to see act two."

HOW TO TELL IF YOU'RE
DEPRESSED: A QUIZ

1 Someone tells you a long, involved, and agoniz-
ing story about a friend of hers who found out
he had cancer after going to the doctor for a head cold.
Your reaction is:
(A) Oh my God! What a horrible story! It's so sad I
just can't stand it! Quick, pass me a tissue!
(B) Cancer. Yes. Well, cancer. I wouldn't mind that
so much. That would be all right. Pretty much the
same as anything else, I guess.

2 You're driving through the most depressing
neighborhood in Queens. Endless dirty-orange
row houses confront your eyes. You immediately think:
(A) The poor sods who have to live here! It must take
them an hour and a half to get to midtown! And what
do they do when they get there? Try to find a parking
space in the Village! See A Chorus Line! Cruise Times
Square and get their wallets snatched! And when they
have to panhandle money to get home again, and
when they finally do get home, it turns out to be here!
(B) Hey, I could live here. I could be pretty happy
here. It would be a nice, quiet life. I would probably
like it.

3 You happen to be passing a church having a
Rummage Sale. At that very moment a man and
a woman laden with bags emerge from the church.

"That was a really wonderful Armani tuxedo, Fred,"

says the woman. "I think you should go back and get it—in perfect condition and only fifty cents."

"I think I will, Susan," says Fred. "And while I'm at it, I'm going to buy you that emerald brooch. After all, it *is* a Tiffany from the twenties. I guess twenty-five dollars isn't too steep."

At this point, do you:

(A) March briskly up to them and say, "Sorry, folks, but I'm from the government's special investigative unit on germ warfare, and there's been a terrible mistake. Some nerve gas has escaped from our laboratory around the corner, nothing serious, it only causes complete memory loss and paralysis in both legs for a year, tops, oh, and then there are the painful boils. Anyway, this is entirely up to you but I would evacuate the immediate vicinity in the next thirty seconds. I'm just going in to tell those nice church ladies."

(B) Think "Who cares?" and keep walking.

To score: If you answered (a) to all the above questions, you are refreshingly healthy and have a good grasp on the essentials of life. If you answered (b) to any or all of the above, you are deeply, clinically depressed and must take drastic measures to restore your sanity.

MORE WAYS TO TELL IF YOU'RE DEPRESSED

• You've dozed off twice while trying to read this sentence.

• Images of severed limbs, copiously bleeding gunshot wounds, and brains spilling onto pavements careen through your dreams.

• Sex, as a concept, seems colorless and dull.

• Your diet consists of tapioca pudding.

• You yawn and hum. Lethargy strikes you halfway up a flight of stairs. Soap operas on TV are too complex and vibrant. You don't answer the phone because you're too busy living on the couch and staring at the ceiling. You *need your rest.*

RITA, JAKE, AND CLEO'S RECOM-MENDED DRASTIC MEASURES TO RESTORE YOUR SANITY

• Unearth whatever you're afraid of. Stare it down, wait it out, dare it to cripple you. Just as a random example, say that your ex-boyfriend is sleeping with someone else. Acknowledge the bottomless pain, then think:

"If I can't cope with this pain, if I run away from it, refuse to acknowledge it, if I run back to him and clasp him around the ankles and make him put on that faded pink T-shirt and sit on the edge of my bed until the end of time, I will never be able to have a real relationship. The fear of abandonment will be my master. If I do anything not to feel abandoned, I will be a wimp, terminally flawed, and forced into dis-self-respectful behavior forever and ever amen."

Those not terrified of losing something are able to keep it.

Or maybe you have lost your job or your home, or something essential has been taken away. Find your way back. Stare the anger and misery down; kill it dead. Everybody loses, everybody dies and puts themselves back together. Hang tough. Let it wash over you but don't drown. Never run away. Trouble is your business.

• A short burst of drug-induced or alcoholic frenzy is desirable, cathartic, and inevitable. But no slow tippling. No gradual deterioration. Destroy your senses only with lust and gusto.

• Picture life as one long hellish journey only punc-tuated by silly men and women dancing pirouettes and playing flutes at the side of the road for no reason. Make those silly men and women your idols.

- Force yourself to exercise. A good way to do this is to go dancing until dawn.
- Spend money. Depression is only for the solvent; it is very expensive. Buy yourself beautiful, high-quality items. Keep doing this until you feel better.
- Take vitamins.
- Change your sheets.
- Spit in somebody's eye.
- Cut self-pity from your repertoire. Ridicule it until it feels humiliated and slinks away.

"That's a good one there, that last one," says Rita. "That might be my favorite."

"Oh shut your gob, you self-righteous Texan slut," I say.

THE *LOW-LIFE I-CHING*

"Good morning, good morning. You are looking bright and perky."

"Mahatma, my sweet angel! Come in. I was just thinking about you."

"I cannot lend you money. I find myself very short at the moment."

"No, no, nothing like that. I just want you to help me. You and I are going to construct the *Low-life I-Ching.*"

"Ah yes. Of course. I see. Huh?"

"You know, Mahatma, I have never worn a love bead in my life. The smell of incense makes me want to shoot someone. And I once vomited when I happened to see a tie-dyed caftan. Yet I love the *I-Ching,* or Book of Changes, with a rare passion."

"Yes, yes," he said, "it is a laudable book. A mystic tome."

"'Pretentious hippy trash psychic mumbo-jumbo, only for passive, mystical neurotics who are afraid to be responsible for their own lives,' a psychiatrist told me once."

"The swine."

"But I told her. 'C. G. Jung, who wrote the foreword to the Richard Wilheim translation, wouldn't agree with you at all,' I said. 'I always knew you were riddled with penis envy and precognitive trauma, but it never occurred to me that you were a moron.' And I marched smartly out of her office, a vision of outraged dignity, and to this day feel perfectly justified in refusing to pay her bill."

"But of course."

You are no doubt aware, dear reader, that the *I-Ching* is an instant Chinese oracle, available to anyone who possesses three coins and the energy to throw them. One throws the coins six times; the order in which they fall leads one inevitably to a hexagram that will explain everything you need to know about you and your life.

The oracle is simply a darling. Polite, mild-mannered, sympathetic, and absolutely lousy with wisdom. Remember those movies they loved in the forties, when an angel would descend from the heavens to tell Jimmy Stewart or somebody what was what? And by the end of the movie Jimmy or somebody would be oozing the milk of human kindness from every pore and his life would be one happy song? The *I-Ching* is just like that angel.

"But because the oracle is so nice and friendly, Mahatma, we tend to abuse our privileges. Have you ever noticed this? Every time a small moment of indecision passes through our brains, we make a beeline to the book, who really has better things to do than tell us which sweater to wear."

"You obviously didn't consult it this morning."

"You don't like my outfit?"

"It is ghastly."

"All the more reason you must help me. For some time now, the world has been crying out for a *Low-life I-Ching*, to help us with those pesky little problems—do I really *need* a new winter coat? Should I become a redhead? Does he like me? Is purple my color? Am I allergic to bean sprouts?—that plague our days."

"Yes, very nice, an interesting idea. I have to go now. I have remembered an urgent appointment." He inched toward the door.

"Get back here, you sorry excuse for a Holy Man. You and I are going to spend however long it takes. We are going to ask the big *I-Ching* to make us a little *I-Ching*."

And we did! It really works; I've been using it for months now. Here it is, the *Low-life I-Ching*. Not enormously good-tempered, not particularly nice, but it will get the job done. Here's how to use it:

1 Make sure your problem is small, almost embarrassingly trivial. The *Low-life I-Ching* is not equipped to deal with the profound, the traumatic, or the transcendental. For those things you must consult the big fellow.

2 After ascertaining that your problem is indeed idiotic, take two coins and throw them four times. If you get two heads or two tails, draw a straight line, *comme ça:*—. If you get one head and one tail, draw a dotted line:--. Start from the bottom and work your way up. Say you get two heads, two tails, a head and a tail, and two tails. Your quatrogram will look like this $\overset{.}{=}\ \overset{}{=}$

3 You will find that your quatrogram closely resembles one contained in the following chart, where each quatrogram is numbered. Match your quatrogram with a number. Go to the text and read what

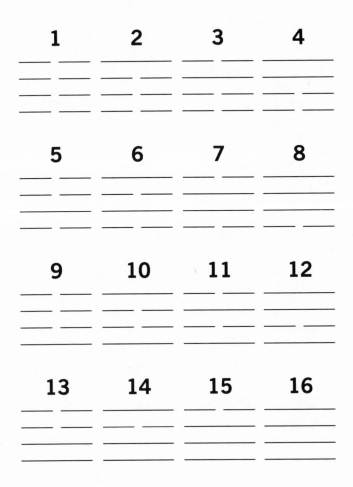

your particular quatrogram says about your problems,
and follow the/its advice.

4 This is not a joke. Well, okay, it's kind of a joke,
but I have used the *Low-life I-Ching* hundreds
of times, and it has only let me down once, when it
told me not to go to this party and then I found out
that Jack Nicholson was there, trying to pick up girls.
Although, who knows, maybe I would have slipped
on a banana peel on the way to the bathroom and
sprained my ankle. That's probably it. Anyway, get
your coins ready; here are your quatrograms:

1. HAVE THE CHICKEN ☰☰

> The knife and fork are at the ready
> The chicken is fragrant
> Eat it before it gets cold

Things are just as they should be. Just make sure
you don't get too fancy or, for that matter, excited.
Your feelings are reciprocated. If you feel like making
a phone call, make it. If you feel like saying "I love
you," say it. You are on your way to success. Even
your unconscious is cooperating in the furthering of
your simple desires toward fulfillment.

But stuff a sock into any grandiose ideas or delusions
of great power. Remain humble, cheerful, unwavering. If you have an urge to move mountains, curb it
until a later date. If you've decided that now is the
time to make a gigantic play for the movie star of your
dreams, you're bonkers.

The chicken is tasty and juicy but essentially a simple, unassuming dish. Eat it gratefully, enjoy its crispy
skin and the richness of its juices, and stop yearning
for beluga with truffles.

2. THE PARTY ANIMAL ☰

Too many martinis
A surfeit of eyeshadow
Are you sure you want to be here?

You may well have got yourself in with the wrong crowd. You, the soul of sociability and bonhomie, may have become deluded by the mists of alcohol or vacant posturings.

Be careful, don't get carried away, remember who you are. One-night stands and fake intimacy are rearing their opportunistic heads. Be polite, make pleasant conversation, but don't plunge headlong into a social situation that is not in your true interests. If you do, the right gang will come along when you're too hung over to notice.

Wait a while. Stay home and wash your hair, do some stretching exercises, brush up on your Italian, read a good book. The right person or group will be making an entrance into your life in the near future. Be ready.

3. CALL YOUR MOTHER ☰

Nonsensical grumblings
Obscure psychological configurations
Look homeward, Angelface

Things are always exactly what they seem, if you know where to look. Can't figure out why you're feeling anxious? Stupified and confused by a significant other's sudden hostilities? A child is acting crazy?

Look to the family, the source of all weirdness. If someone's getting out of hand, running riot, throwing tantrums, it will make sense if you delve, deep and clear, back to origins.

Don't act wildly, don't do anything stupid, don't let anybody get away with anything. Make sure you're right, then act.

4. SOMEBODY'S BEING SILLY

Hair ribbons and frills
Tears before bedtime
Forgive them when you can

There are times when humans act badly, not from malice but from stupidity. Have you? Has somebody else? A little maturity is needed at the moment. Idiocy can be grown out of; change is possible if not probable.

You have two choices: Either look the other way, gloss it over, it's not important. A little acting out never hurt anybody; forgive, forget.

But if you're *really* angry and dealing with someone incorrigible, punish him in a cool, deliberate manner. Make the punishment fit the crime. Be calm. Receptive. Adorable.

5. DON'T GET CUTE

The designer coat is out the window
Put on the down vest
And keep cool

Lean, mean times. No showing off at the moment. Mellow out, lay back, keep it simple. As long as you don't put on any airs or start spinning fancy yarns about how your family is in oil but your trust fund is tied up, or you're not sure but you've heard you're next in line for the Nobel peace prize, you'll be fine.

This is no time to get either angry or carried away by lust. Well, maybe a little lust. But be careful; make sure you know who you're fondling.

10. GO OUT FOR DINNER ☰

Pump those muscles
Rush headlong
Fear no weirdness

Be strong, be sure, be powerful, be swift, be tall.
Get out of the house, make your presence seen, heard,
felt. Wear your best clothes, your sharpest wit, go for
it.

No retiring shyly into corners, no staying home to
rinse out your socks. Don't be afraid of making an ass
of yourself; you probably will, but no one will care.
They will think you charming and vulnerable and
cute.

There may be a small contretemps. Pay it no mind;
everybody's just kidding.

11. JUMPING THE GUN ☰

Drug-induced insights
One-night stands
Where do they get you?

Take a chill, pill, if you have the will to be still.
Cool out, calm down, lay back. Things are going along
very nicely, thank you very much, and will continue
to do so as long as you don't turn all hyper and demand
instant gratification.

Keep things moving, but slowly. Slowly. Don't be-
moan your lack of progress; your life is not a rock
video. Things are moving at a snail's pace, but they
are moving. Nothing sudden is lasting. Keep chipping
away; you'll get there by and by.

12. LOOK UP ☰

The moon, almost full
A party dress
Time for a giggle

Make sure you're not on any high horses. The stars we're concerned with exist in the sky, not behind the doors of some glittering nightclub. It is possible to fall in love with someone Liz Smith has never heard of. It is often preferable. Don't be vapid and take the short, or starfucker's, view. Remember what's important.

Then make a few phone calls. You've been stewing too long and need to get out and talk to people. You're pale from self-abuse. Time for an influx of new ideas; this will help you sort out previous misconceptions. You don't want to turn into one of those people who won't join any club that will have you as a member.

13. HEAD FOR THE HILLS ☰

Naval contemplation goes awry
By your acts they will know you
Take a long drive

The truth must be faced: You are not the center of the universe. A bitter pill to swallow, but hurry up, it's transition time.

You're heading for a change. Here's how to do it: Stop eating breakfast at the same old coffee shop, cease your activities at cocktail parties. The pictures you're getting are confused.

Drive into the literal or figurative mountains and check into a hotel. Think, put things into perspective, avoid like the plague your own egotism. .There are many other points of view. Avoid self-absorption and consider the effect you have on others. You do—people look to you for guidance, for approval, for a good joke. Take yourself in hand and your progress will be strong and sure.

14.   THE CHECK IS IN THE MAIL

> The weirdness is passing
> Twitch those curtains open
> A sunny day at last

Yes, you have been frazzled by difficulties. Your poor friends haven't known what to do with you. They take you to the movies and you scratch your head and burst into tears. Tensions and complications.

Liberation is at hand. Things are starting to return to normal. People have been rude or even horrible, but forgive them; everybody is an asshole some of the time, even you.

Go to the post office, take those dirty clothes to the laundry, thank God you can again be normal. But be careful not to push it. Don't overdo your triumph or you'll undo yourself.

15.   BURN-OUT, START AGAIN

> Cries and whispers
> A judicious temper tantrum
> Take your toys and go home

Intimations of your own mortality can make you crazy if you let them. You know how you can go on a three-day maniacal bender; you know how you can consume yourself with melancholy while eating a dozen chocolate bars.

Life isn't fair, life is sad, nobody said it was going to be easy. But don't throw yourself off your own roof. You may simply be suffering from advanced PMS, middle-aged crisis, or the syndrome of too-much-too-soon-for-no-apparent-reason.

Curb your restlessness, have a good cry; good fortune flies out of the floods of grief. Your heart will change. It has to. Time to start over. Find your place by both separating and uniting and all will be aces.

16.   ONE LEG AT A TIME

> Try a little tenderness
> Penetrate politely
> Block that kick!

What we need here is sweetness and gentleness coupled with the unwavering singlemindedness of an MX missile.

Keep moving; you're in danger of crippling yourself with your own indecision. You're thinking yourself into a welter of confusion. Options are multiplying; take care not to be driven off course and into the quagmire.

Act or solidify. Free yourself of those self-aggrandizing fits of pique and stave off paralysis. Listen to a really great record that makes you dance and realize the meaning of life. Dance with a stranger. Grab your darling and drive down the highway at a hundred miles an hour.

REASONS TO BE CHEERFUL

The Kiwi, walking down Seventh Avenue, watched four girls cruise by in a red convertible.

"Don't wave," I said.

"Who would wave?" said Cleo.

"He's wearing a fake leather jacket made out of some desperately ugly foam-stuff," said Lucy.

"You can call that at fifty feet?" asked Rita, who was

driving. "If this light doesn't change soon he'll be upon us."

The Kiwi, on his way to buy wheat-grass juice, walked indecisively. He started to come toward the car, wobbled away again, walked toward the car again, then the light changed.

"Gun it," said Cleo.

"Maybe I should have talked to him," I said.

"You need to get your perspective back first," said Rita. "That will take approximately ten weeks."

"From now?"

"Definitely. Addictions are relentless."

"So I had this dream last night—wait, here's the turn to the tunnel—I was in the kitchen doing the dishes, and I spied a plate of leftovers, which I examined carefully. Then I walked into the other room and said, "Okay, who left her diaphragm in the scalloped potatoes?"

"And who did?" wondered Lucy.

"Cleo. She was so cool, she walked casually into the other room and retrieved it."

"Naturally," said Cleo. "This dream reveals that you are rediscovering your sense of reality."

An hour later, speeding along the countryside of the north shore of Long Island, I shrieked, "Wait! Wait!"

Rita screeched to a halt. "What? What?"

I pointed fervently to a sign in front of a Presbyterian church, which said "Rummage sale today."

Rita parked, Lucy got out of the car while it was still moving and ran into the church. By the time we arrived, she was already clutching a black silk slip, a chintz-covered chair cushion, three embroidered hankies, and a silver charm bracelet.

I wrenched the chintz cushion out of her arms, while Cleo took peremptory possession of the charm bracelet. We let her keep the rest.

I looked around and inhaled deeply. The sight and

smell of a church rummage sale is better for me than a thousand shrinks telling me it was all my mother's fault, better than Robert Redford confessing his love, better than a swim in any ocean, better than any single sexual episode I can think of—except three good ones put together. A church rummage sale is full of infinite pleasures and possibilities, mystical, healing, calm, and joyous.

The church was old with gleaming wood and lofty ceilings, the air was cool and thick with an evocative musty smell. In a state of divine contemplation, I went through stacks of sheets, boxes of gloves, piles of lingerie, cartons of bow ties. Occasionally I caught sight of one of the other girls similarly transformed. In the midst of my reverie I heard a voice.

"You're my kind of woman," the voice said.

I looked around, saw nothing.

"It's the way you go through every box, looking behind and under things, ablaze with curiosity."

I looked around, saw nobody, started having notions about Allen Funt. And then there he was, behind a stack of Reader's Digest condensed books, glaring shyly at the floor.

He was an old man with grizzled gray hair, about seventy-five, wearing overalls and a flannel shirt. He was hugely embarrassed at having spoken and refused to take his eyes from a beam of pink light cast by the stained-glass windows.

"Look," I said inanely as I held up my hands, "green suede gloves. Fifty cents."

"Used to belong to Eulalia Henderson," he replied, "who was a devil with the men in her prime. Died last year at eighty-five."

"Think they'll bring me luck?"

He looked up at me furtively. His eyes were pale green. "I used to be a physicist," he said. "Knew everything. Gave it up. Over in that pile there you'll find a tea towel embroidered with spaceships and puppies. You'll like that."

"I guess you do know everything," I said upon discovering the tea towel.

"You also got a sad, lonely look in your eye," he said. "This worries me."

"Look! Orange heels!" I heard Rita yell from across the room.

"Here's something I know," said the old man. "I know that even the physicists have discovered chaos. That's what the big guys study now—the Chaos Theory."

"Meaning?"

"Meaning that nothing is predictable. They got a whole bunch of military fellows sniffing after the chaos guys—the military fellows think the chaos guys will help them control the propellers on their helicopters and make star wars work. Hah! Nothing in the universe is predictable. So there's no point in you having that fatal look in your eye."

"I've lost my true love, my little boy is growing up and will soon leave home, one of my best friends is desperately ill, the world seems strange and ugly, and I'm feeling tired and feeble and weird."

"Ah, chicken-shit," he said. "Come on, let's take a walk." He led me into the graveyard of the church, which was cool, leafy, and bright.

"Here's my Sadie," he said, pointing proudly to an ivy-covered grave. "She's happy. I'm happier, I'm still alive. Who knows what's going to happen next? Today I met you. And you look like you've got the capacity for about three more true loves, about ten more children who'll up and leave like they're supposed to, and a hundred more sick friends. You have to have faith. Walk around those blind corners."

"Are we entering into a religious discussion here?" I asked fishily.

"Hell, I doubt it. Having fallen in love with a young red-headed woman wearing Eulalia Henderson's gloves, I'm just shooting the breeze."

"Here's all I know," I said, plucking a blade of

crabgrass and turning it, with a series of complex and sophisticated maneuvers, into a whistle, "There are certain tricks. One trick is not forgetting a thing. The way a child's hair falls over his nose when he's flipping baseball cards. The way the sweat beads on a lover's brow when he's lying. The way a mother turns her back, a friend tells her secrets."

"Are you out there, you lamebrain?" I heard Cleo yelling.

"Here's what I know," the man said. "If we lived in a microscopic world, trucks would crash into walls, fly apart, and then reassemble perfectly on the other side of the wall. This has been proven."

"Have faith, hey?"

"Have faith in your own sinew, your nerve endings. Stop talking to an old man in a graveyard and go out and kick some ass," he said.

"I'm already gone," I said.